HENRIK IBSEN

Born in Norway in 1828, Ibsen began his writing career with romantic history plays influenced by Shakespeare and Schiller. In 1851 he was appointed writer-in-residence at the newly established Norwegian Theatre in Bergen with a contract to write a play a year for five years, following which he was made artistic director of the Norwegian Theatre in what is now Oslo. In the 1860s he moved abroad to concentrate wholly on writing. He began with two mighty verse dramas, *Brand* and *Peer Gynt,* and in the 1870s and '80s wrote the sequence of realistic 'problem' plays for which he is best known, among them *A Doll's House, Ghosts, An Enemy of the People* and *Hedda Gabler.* His last four plays, *The Master Builder, Little Eyolf, John Gabriel Borkman* and *When We Dead Awaken,* dating from his return to Norway in the 1890s, are increasingly overlaid with symbolism. Illness forced him to retire in 1900, and he died in 1906 after a series of crippling strokes.

RICHARD EYRE

Having spent five years each at the Royal Lyceum, Edinburgh, and Nottingham Playhouse, Richard Eyre was Artistic Director of the National Theatre from 1988 to 1997, where he directed, amongst others, Daniel Day-Lewis in *Hamlet,* Ian McKellen in *Richard III,* Ian Holm in *King Lear,* and Paul Scofield in *John Gabriel Borkman,* as well as the David Hare Trilogy, *Skylight, Amy's View, The Invention of Love, Vincent in Brixton,* and *Guys and Dolls.* Other productions include *Jingo* (RSC), *Edmond, Kafka's Dick* (Royal Court), *The Judas Kiss* (Almeida/Broadway), *The Crucible* on Broadway and *Mary Poppins* in the West End. Television and film work includes *The Ploughman's Lunch, Tumbledown, Suddenly Last Summer, The Absence of War, Stage Beauty* and *Iris,* based on John Bailey's memoirs of Iris Murdoch, for which he also co-wrote the screenplay. Publications include *Utopia and Other Places, Changing Stages,* co-written with Nicholas Wright to accompany his BBC television series of the same name, and *National Service,* chronicling his time at the National Theatre. He was knighted in 1997.

HENRIK IBSEN

HEDDA GABLER

in a new version by
RICHARD EYRE

from a literal translation by
Karin and Ann Bamborough

with an Introduction by Richard Eyre

NICK HERN BOOKS
London

www.nickhernbooks.co.uk

To S and L

A Nick Hern Book

This version of *Hedda Gabler* first published in Great Britain
as a paperback original in 2005 by Nick Hern Books Limited,
14 Larden Road, London W3 7ST

This version of *Hedda Gabler* by Richard Eyre copyright © 2005
Chestermead Ltd

Introduction by Richard Eyre copyright © 2005 Chestermead Ltd

This version is from a literal translation by Karin and Ann Bamborough

Richard Eyre has asserted his right to be identified as author of this
version

Cover image: Eve Best as Hedda, Almeida Theatre, 2005.
Photograph by Allan Titmuss

Typeset by Country Setting, Kingsdown, Kent, CT14 8ES
Printed in Great Britain by Cox and Wyman Ltd, Reading, Berks

A CIP record for this book is available from the British Library

ISBN 1 85459 842 2

Introduction

It's a paradox of great plays, which are great on account of the profound specificity of their characters and actions, that we try to compress them into neat, autographed theses, hoping that our mark on them will be as lasting as handprints on drying cement rather than sand in the incoming tide. We provide ourselves with generalised conceits – *King Lear* is 'about' fatherhood, *Richard III* is 'about' tyranny, *Hedda Gabler* is 'about' the position of women – which shrivel the beguiling complexities and ambiguities that have drawn us to the plays in the first place. Great plays are great precisely because, to borrow King Lear's words, they show us the 'mystery of things' rather than serve as tools for polemic or guides to good living.

That Hedda is a victim (tragic or not) of her gender and social conditions – and of her own self-destructiveness – is unquestionable, and it's quite reasonable to conscript her to the ranks of fighters for the freedom of women while characterising the men in her life as her oppressors; in short, to argue that the play is 'about' feminism and patriarchy.

But part of what is so alluring – and daring – about *Hedda Gabler* is its wit, its unexpected lack of solemnity, its defiance of an audience's expectations, its reluctance to conform to reductive theory. Is there any other dramatic heroine who possesses such an extraordinary confection of characteristics as Hedda? She's feisty, droll and intelligent, yet fatally ignorant of the world and herself. She's snobbish, mean-spirited, small-minded, conservative, cold, bored, vicious; sexually eager but terrified of sex, ambitious to be bohemian but frightened of scandal, a desperate romantic fantasist but unable to sustain any loving relationship with anyone, including herself. And yet, in spite of all this, she mesmerises us and compels our pity.

Hedda can't even succeed in dominating the centre of the universe she has created: in the 36 hours of the action of the play she realises that as a mere wife of an academic, she's powerless, imprisoned by her prospective motherhood and indentured to a cruel man as his mistress. Suicide is the only way out, a final, awful, 'grand gesture'.

'The title of the play,' said Ibsen in a letter, 'is *Hedda Gabler* [rather than 'Hedda Tesman' – her husband's name]. I intended to indicate thereby that as a personality she is to be regarded rather as her father's daughter than as her husband's wife.' Hedda's father was a general, with the status if not the wealth of an aristocrat and, according to Ibsen's notes, Hedda was born when her father was already an old man and had left the army in slightly discreditable circumstances. Hedda, an orphan (perhaps the mother died in childbirth), is left to vindicate her father's reputation. 'She really wants to live the whole life of a *man,*' said Ibsen, but of course, as he said in his notes for *A Doll's House*: 'A woman cannot be herself in modern society. It is an exclusively male society, with laws made by men and with prosecutors and judges who assess feminine conduct from a masculine standpoint.'

Which might suggest a schematic creation of a character, but Hedda seems a creation as ambiguous and unpredictable as anyone you might meet in life – and, in the case of a Hedda, avoid. And to her creator she, and indeed everyone in the play, were as real as if they had lived: 'Finally, in the last draft, I have reached the limit of my knowledge; I know my characters from close and long acquaintance – they are my intimate friends, who will no longer disappoint me; as I see them now, I shall always see them.'

That quality of even-handedly creating characters who seem to exist independently of their maker is not one that I, at least, have often ascribed to Ibsen. It's more, well, a Chekhovian quality and perhaps it's a confession of ignorance (or banality) that for many years I thought a liking for Chekhov and for Ibsen were incompatible: you declared yourself for one party or the other. 'Ibsen is an idiot,' said Chekhov and in my infatuation I was prepared to agree with him. But compare these two statements:

'It was not really my intention to deal in this play with so-called problems. What I principally wanted to do was to depict human beings, human emotions, and human destinies, upon a groundwork of certain of the social conditions and principles of the present day.'

'You are right in demanding that an artist approach his work consciously, but you are confusing two concepts: the solution of a problem and the correct formulation of a problem. Only the second is required of the artist.'

And then answer the question: which is Chekhov, which Ibsen? (The first is Ibsen.)

When I was working with the conductor, Georg Solti, I asked him what he regretted most: 'Not being able to say sorry to Shostakovich for having under-rated him and thought of him as a lackey of the state.' I've often felt I'd like to apologise to Ibsen for my prejudice. I have a temperamental inclination to Chekhov because of his mordant wit and wordliness, his doctor's eye and his talent for transforming experience of life and love into art. But in fact, at least as far as *Hedda Gabler* is concerned, Ibsen was doing the same thing. 'The essential thing,' he said, 'is . . . to draw a clear distinction between what one has merely experienced and what one has spiritually *lived through*; for only the latter is proper material for creative writing.'

It's both pointless and prurient to behave as if there's a linear equation that connects life (particularly love-life) and art, but in the case of *Hedda Gabler* there's no question that events in Ibsen's life were a catalyst to his creative process, a crystal of lived experience around which the play coalesced.

In the summer of 1889, when he was 61, Ibsen was on holiday in a South Tyrolean village. He met an 18-year-old Viennese girl called Emilie Bardach and fell in love. He'd dedicated himself to his art like a monk, for 'the power and the glory', and he'd renounced spontaneous joy and sexual fulfilment. Emilie became the 'May sun of a September life'. She asked him to live with her; he at first agreed but, crippled by guilt and fear of scandal (and perhaps impotence as well), put an end to the relationship.

Emilie, like Hedda, was a beautiful, intelligent, spoilt, bored upper-class girl with 'a tired look in her mysterious eyes', who wanted to have power and was thrilled at the possibility of snaring someone else's husband. The village in which they met in the Tyrol – Gossensass – was mentioned specifically in an earlier draft of the play when Hedda and Loevborg are looking at the honeymoon photographs in the second act, and fragments of dialogue in Ibsen's notes from the play appear to be derived directly from his conversations with Emilie.

But, if Emilie was the inspiration for the character of Hedda, Ibsen himself – consciously or not – contributed many of her characteristics. With his fear of scandal and ridicule, his apparent repulsion with the reality of sex, his yearning for an emotional freedom, Ibsen might have said of Hedda, as Flaubert did of Madame Bovary: 'Hedda, c'est moi.'

There were two entirely unconnected events which occurred last year that drew my attention to the play. I was sitting in a dentist's waiting room reading an interview in *Hello!* magazine with a rich posh young woman who was celebrated for being celebrated. She craved attention and yet had no talent for anything but self-advertisement and was quoted, without irony (never the strong suit of *Hello!*), as saying: 'I'm afraid I have a great talent for boredom.'

Mmmm, I thought, Hedda Gabler lives. The same evening I went to a fine production of Eugene O'Neill's *Mourning Becomes Electra* and saw an actress, Eve Best, who seemed born to play Hedda. With the sort of credulousness typical of a reader of *Hello!,* I took the synchronicity as a sign that I should do the play and got myself commissioned by Robert Fox and by Michael Attenborough at the Almeida Theatre to do a new translation.

The best way of understanding a play is to write it – even if that means merely typing a script yourself or copying out in longhand. It obliges you to question the meaning of every word, speech, gesture and stage direction. Arthur Miller once said to me: 'You know what I used to do years ago? I would take any of Shakespeare's plays and simply copy them. Pretending that I was him, you see. You know, it's a marvellous exercise. Just copy the speeches, and you gradually realise the concision, the packing together of experience, which is hard to do just with your ear, but if you have to work it with a pen or a piece of paper and you see that stuff coming together in that intense inner connection of sound and meaning.'

Which is what I've tried to do in this version of Ibsen's great play. It can't properly be called a 'translation' because I speak not a word of Norwegian. I worked from a literal version by Karin and Ann Bamborough, and I tried to animate the language in a way that felt as true as possible to what I understood from them to be the author's intentions – even to the point of trying to capture cadences that I could at least infer from the Norwegian original. But even literal translations make choices and the choices we make are made according to taste, to the times we live in and how we view the world. All choices are choices of meaning, of intention. What I have written is a 'version' or 'adaptation' or 'interpretation' of Ibsen's play, but I hope that it comes close to squaring the circle of being close to what Ibsen intended while seeming spontaneous to an audience of today.

Richard Eyre
February 2005

Characters

HEDDA TESMAN, *daughter of General Gabler, twenty-nine*

GEORGE TESMAN, *her husband, an academic, thirty-three*

JULIANA TESMAN, *his aunt, sixty-five*

JUDGE BRACK, *circuit judge, forty-five*

EILERT LOEVBORG, *writer, thirty-three*

THEA ELVSTED, *wife of a High Sheriff, twenty-six*

BERTHE, *maid, fifty-five*

This version of *Hedda Gabler* was first performed at the
Almeida Theatre, London, on 10 March 2005, with the
following cast:

HEDDA TESMAN	Eve Best
GEORGE TESMAN	Benedict Cumberbatch
JULIANA TESMAN	Gillian Raine
JUDGE BRACK	Iain Glen
EILERT LOEVBORG	Jamie Sives
THEA ELVSTED	Lisa Dillon
BERTHE	Sarah Flind

Director   Richard Eyre
Designer   Rob Howell
Lighting designer   Peter Mumford
Sound designer   John Leonard

Thanks to Michael Attenborough and Robert Fox.   R.E.

ACT ONE

A large, elegant, well-furnished, contemporary (1890) drawing room: a sofa, a round table and chairs, an armchair and footstool by a large porcelain stove, an upright piano. Fine carpets. It's a room clearly intended for entertaining. A smaller room lies beyond, where a large portrait of a good-looking military officer can be seen. There are fresh flowers in vases and bouquets on tables all over the room.

Morning light floods through French windows. It's autumn.

A small woman in her mid-sixties, MISS TESMAN, *tiptoes into the room. She's wearing a hat and carrying a parasol. She's followed by a plump middle-aged woman,* BERTHE, *the maid, who is carrying a bunch of flowers.*

MISS TESMAN (*whispering*). Well . . . I don't think they're up yet.

BERTHE (*whispering*). 'S'what I said. Still, the boat was late wa'n it and – God – the stuff she wanted to unpack before she'd go to bed.

MISS TESMAN. Well, let's have some fresh air to welcome them.

She opens the French windows. BERTHE *looks to her for advice, shrugs and puts the flowers on the piano.*

BERTHE (*in tears*). I don't know where to put nothing.

MISS TESMAN. Berthe . . . It broke my heart to lose you.

BERTHE. I worked for you and your sister for . . .

MISS TESMAN. I know, dear, but there's no alternative. George needs you, he must have you, you've been looking after him since he was little.

BERTHE. What with poor Miss Rena being sick – she can't do for herself at all . . .

MISS TESMAN. Oh, I'll manage.

BERTHE. . . . and I might not be up to scratch for Georgie's
    wife, I mean for Miss Hedda, Mrs Tesman, I mean . . .

MRS ELVSTED. At the beginning there's bound –

BERTHE. . . . she can be quite mardy, I've heard.

MISS TESMAN. Well, she's a general's daughter, she's used
    to fine things and things just so. That black riding dress, you
    remember . . . She used to ride out with her father –

BERTHE. With a feather in her hat like the Queen of Sheba.
    Never thought Georgie'd –

MISS TESMAN. Berthe, you must call him '*Doctor*' now.

BERTHE. Doctor. Aye. She said that last night. Just as soon as
    she stepped in the door.

MISS TESMAN. They made him a doctor in Germany. 'I'm
    Doctor Tesman now, Aunt Juju!' he told me when he came
    down the gangway.

BERTHE. He could be whatever he wanted. Mind, I never had
    him for a medical man, too dainty for that . . .

MISS TESMAN. No no, he's not that sort of doctor, Lord no.
    But he might have an even more important title soon . . .

BERTHE. What's that, then?

MISS TESMAN (*smiling, she puts her finger to her lips*).
    Mum. If only my sweet brother could have lived to see –
    (*She stops.*) Berthe?

BERTHE. Miss Juju?

MISS TESMAN. What have you done?

BERTHE. Miss Juju?

MISS TESMAN. You've taken the covers off the furniture.

BERTHE. Madam said I should. Said she couldn't be doing
    with covers on furniture.

MISS TESMAN. But they can't be going to use this room for
    every day . . .

BERTHE. Madam is. Georgie – the Doctor – didn't say.

GEORGE TESMAN *comes into the back room holding an
    empty, open suitcase. He's a young-looking 33, round-faced,
    glasses, bearded, a little plump, casually dressed.*

MISS TESMAN. Good *morning,* George.

TESMAN. Aunt Juju. You're so early and you must be so tired.

MISS TESMAN. I had to see you settled in . . .

TESMAN. And all the way from the port last night, there and back, no?

MISS TESMAN. It's good for me.

TESMAN. We were so sorry we couldn't take you in the carriage . . .

MISS TESMAN. Oh, goodness, the Judge looked after me, he saw me home.

TESMAN. Hedda's bags were . . .

MISS TESMAN. *What* a mountain! I've *never* seen such a . . . mountain.

BERTHE. Shall I help Madam?

TESMAN. No, you're not to disturb her. She'll ring if she wants you.

BERTHE *starts to go.*

Oh, take this will you, Berthe?

BERTHE. I'll put it in the attic.

BERTHE *goes out.*

TESMAN. Amazing, Aunt Juju, that case was crammed with papers. Incredible, what I found. The archives, you know, in the museums. Notes, documents – things people didn't know existed, I even found –

MISS TESMAN. You didn't waste your time on your honeymoon.

TESMAN. Not a moment. Oh Aunt Juju, do take your hat off. Here, let me, yes?

MISS TESMAN (*as he takes the hat off*). Dear Georgie . . . it's like being at home.

TESMAN. Lovely hat, Aunt Juju.

MISS TESMAN. It's for Hedda.

TESMAN. Hedda?

MISS TESMAN. So she won't be ashamed of me if we're ever walking together.

TESMAN (*stroking her cheek*). Aunt Juju, you're a marvel. Let's chat before Hedda appears.

He puts the hat down on an armchair. She puts her parasol in the corner of the sofa. She takes both his hands in hers and they sit side by side.

MISS TESMAN. Dear Georgie, you're the living image of my dear brother. I feel safe now, it's such a blessing to have you back with us.

TESMAN. It is for me, you're my family, Aunt Juju, you and Aunt Rena.

MISS TESMAN. And I know you'll go on caring for us, even, well . . .

TESMAN. She's no better?

MISS TESMAN (*tearful*). She's . . . I hope she lasts longer, I don't know what I'd do without her now I haven't got you to look after.

TESMAN (*patting her back*). You'll always have me.

MISS TESMAN (*pulling herself together*). No, you've got a wife now. Imagine, George. You went off with Hedda Gabler, and she had *so* many admirers.

TESMAN *gets up, stretches his legs.*

TESMAN. Hmmm . . . I think there are quite a few men who'd like to be me, no?

MISS TESMAN. *Such* a honeymoon, Georgie. You've been away nearly six months.

TESMAN. Well, I was studying and doing research. And I had a lot of reading to do.

MISS TESMAN (*whispering*). Do you have any *news*?

TESMAN. What news?

MISS TESMAN. *News.*

TESMAN. I wrote you everything. I told you last night I'd got my doctorate.

MISS TESMAN. I mean *news*.

TESMAN. News?

MISS TESMAN. Oh Georgie, I'm your aunt, news of the *future*.

TESMAN. Oh, yes, yes of course I do.

MISS TESMAN. And?

TESMAN. Well, I could . . . I could become a professor soon.

MISS TESMAN. Yes but –

TESMAN. But you know that. It's pretty well certain.

MISS TESMAN. Yes. Yes, of course.

Pause.

And what about the cost, Georgie?

TESMAN. Of the honeymoon? Well, the grant helped a lot.

MISS TESMAN. For the two of you, I don't know how . . .

TESMAN (*laughing*). I don't know how either.

MISS TESMAN. With a dashing young lady.

TESMAN. She had to have the trip, Aunt, she just had to. It would have been wrong not to do it for her.

MISS TESMAN. Well, I suppose it's the fashion nowadays, isn't it? And have you had a chance to look round the house?

TESMAN. I got up as soon as it was light.

MISS TESMAN. And what do you think?

TESMAN. It's wonderful. Wonderful. But I've no idea what we're going to do with the extra rooms.

MISS TESMAN (*chuckling*). Oh, you'll find a use.

TESMAN. My library?

MISS TESMAN (*straight-faced*). Of course, George, of course for your library.

TESMAN. Hedda said she would never want to live anywhere but here . . .

MISS TESMAN. . . . and it came up for sale.

TESMAN. What luck, no?

MISS TESMAN. But so *expensive*, Georgie.

TESMAN. Do you think so?

MISS TESMAN. *Lord*, yes!

He sits next to her.

TESMAN. Very, do you think?

MISS TESMAN. Well, the bills haven't come in yet, dear.

TESMAN. Thank God Brack managed to negotiate such favourable terms. He wrote to Hedda about it.

MISS TESMAN. You mustn't worry, I've stood security for the furniture and rugs.

TESMAN. What security? What do you mean?

MISS TESMAN. My annuity.

TESMAN. From your trust fund? You and Aunt Rena?

MISS TESMAN. It's a mortgage, you see.

He jumps up.

TESMAN. It's the only money you've got!

MISS TESMAN. It's just a formality. The Judge arranged it for me. A mere formality, he said . . .

TESMAN. Well, it may be but –

MISS TESMAN. You've got your own salary for now and we wanted to help anyway.

TESMAN. You're always sacrificing yourself for me.

She gets up and puts her hands on his shoulders.

MISS TESMAN. Georgie . . . dear Georgie, have I got any other pleasure left than to make your life easier? Things might have been hard for you, my little orphan, but now you're there. You're at the top, George.

He shrugs diffidently, smiling.

TESMAN. Things really do seem to have worked out.

MISS TESMAN. And the people who tried to make things difficult for you, well, they can just . . . they can just *bow down* to you, George.

TESMAN. Oh Auntie . . .

MISS TESMAN. No, George, that man who was your rival,
that misbegotten creature, he's just lying in the dirt now.
And it's what he deserves.

TESMAN. Have you heard anything of him recently?

MISS TESMAN. He's supposed to have a new book out.

TESMAN. Eilert has? Eilert Loevborg?

MISS TESMAN. I can't think it can be up to much. Now,
when *your* book comes out, that'll be something. What's the
subject?

TESMAN. It'll be about life in the Brabant – that's Holland –
in the Middle Ages, more specifically the domestic
industries, that's the people who worked from their 'homes',
the craftsmen and –

MISS TESMAN. Imagine being able to write about such
things!

TESMAN. I've got a lot of cataloguing and research to do
before I start writing.

MISS TESMAN. You're not my brother's son for nothing.

TESMAN. I can't wait to get going now I'm in my own home.

MISS TESMAN. With the girl of your dreams.

He embraces her.

TESMAN. She's the best thing in my life, Aunt Juju. (*He
hears footsteps.*) Hedda? No?

HEDDA *appears in the back room. She's a tallish, striking,
aristocratic-looking woman of 29. Pale face; cold, clear and
calm grey eyes. Quite short, thin brown hair. Dressed in a
stylish dressing-gown.*

MISS TESMAN. Hedda, dear! Good *morning*!

HEDDA. Miss Tesman, good morning. It's kind of you to visit
so early.

MISS TESMAN. Well, I . . . Did you sleep well in your new
house?

HEDDA. Not bad, thank you.

TESMAN (*laughs*). Not bad? You were sleeping like a stone when I got up.

HEDDA. Mercifully. But it just goes to show that one can get used to all novelty, doesn't it, Miss Tesman? Bit by bit. God, the maid's left the windows open, there's a whole *sea* of sun.

MISS TESMAN (*going towards the windows*). Well, let's just close them, shall we?

HEDDA. No, no, leave them. Tesman, be a dear, close the shutters, the light's blinding.

TESMAN (*closing the shutters*). There. Now you've got fresh air *and* shade.

HEDDA. Yes, fresh air, that's what we need in here . . . all these frightful flowers. I'm so sorry, won't you sit down, Miss Tesman?

MISS TESMAN. Thank you so much, but I'd better be getting back now I know that all is well here. Back to my dear patient.

TESMAN. Give her my love. Tell her I'll be over later today.

MISS TESMAN. Of course I will . . . Oh, I almost forgot, this is for you.

She fumbles in her bag and hands him a flat package wrapped in newspaper.

TESMAN. What is it?

MISS TESMAN. Look.

TESMAN (*opening it*). Oh Aunt Juju. You kept them, that's so sweet. Hedda, look!

HEDDA (*not looking*). What?

TESMAN. My slippers!

HEDDA. The ones you were pining for when we were away.

TESMAN (*crossing to her*). Look, you can see them in the flesh.

HEDDA (*moving away*). No, thank you.

TESMAN (*following her*). Aunt Rena embroidered them, in spite of being ill. They've got such sentimental value.

HEDDA. Not for me.

MISS TESMAN. I'm sure Hedda's right, George.

TESMAN. No, she's part of our family now, she's –

HEDDA. I don't think this maid'll do.

MISS TESMAN. Berthe?

TESMAN. What do you mean?

HEDDA. Look, she's left her old hat on the chair.

HEDDA points at MISS TESMAN*'s hat.* TESMAN, *shocked and frightened, drops his slippers.*

TESMAN. Hedda –

HEDDA. What if we had guests?

TESMAN. Hedda, that's Aunt Juju's hat.

HEDDA. Is it?

MISS TESMAN (*taking it*). It is. And it isn't old, thank you very much, Madame Hedda.

HEDDA (*shrugs*). I just glanced at it.

MISS TESMAN (*putting the hat on*). It's the first time I've worn it. And that's God's truth.

TESMAN. And it's a very handsome hat. Really . . . *chic*.

MISS TESMAN. Don't get carried away, George dear. Where's my parasol? (*Taking it, she mutters:*) That's not Berthe's either.

TESMAN. New hat, new parasol. Look, Hedda.

HEDDA. Lovely.

TESMAN. Lovely is what you are, Hedda. Look, Auntie, isn't she lovely?

MISS TESMAN. Well, *that's* nothing new, she's been lovely all her life.

She has started for the door.

TESMAN. But not pink and healthy and putting on weight.

HEDDA. Oh, do stop it!

MISS TESMAN. Putting on weight?

TESMAN. You can't see now, but I can testify to –

HEDDA. You can't testify to anything.

TESMAN. The air in Austria –

HEDDA. I haven't changed a jot.

TESMAN. That's what you keep saying, but you're wrong, isn't she, Aunt Juju?

MISS TESMAN *looks at* HEDDA *for a moment.*

MISS TESMAN. You are lovely. Hedda is lovely.

MISS TESMAN *goes to her, takes her head between her hands and kisses the top of her head.*

Bless you, Hedda Tesman. For George's sake.

HEDDA (*gently breaking free*). *Please* . . .

MISS TESMAN (*with quiet conviction*). I'll be seeing the two of you every day.

TESMAN. Do, Aunt Juju. No?

MISS TESMAN. Goodbye. Till tomorrow.

She goes out. TESMAN *can be heard thanking his aunt for the slippers.* HEDDA *paces furiously, raising her arms and clenching her fists. She opens the shutters of the French windows and stares out.* TESMAN *comes back in.*

TESMAN. What are you looking at?

HEDDA. The leaves. They're yellow. And withered.

TESMAN. We are in September.

HEDDA. Yes, we are in September.

TESMAN. Didn't you think Aunt Juju seemed rather odd? Rather . . . withdrawn? Do you think there was something wrong, no?

HEDDA. I've no idea, I don't know her. Isn't she always like that?

TESMAN. Not really . . .

HEDDA (*looking at him*). You think she was offended by the thing with the hat.

TESMAN. Perhaps just for a moment.

HEDDA. Well, what sort of behaviour is it to throw your hat on the furniture in the drawing room? One doesn't do that.

TESMAN. I'm sure she won't do it again.

HEDDA. Anyway, I'll be nice to her.

TESMAN. Would you, Hedda?

HEDDA. You can ask her here when you see her later.

TESMAN. I will, and it would make her day if you'd call her Aunt Juju, Hedda.

HEDDA. I've told you, Tesman, I will call her 'Aunt' if I must, but that's as far as I'll go.

TESMAN. I just thought as a member of the family . . .

HEDDA *shakes her head vigorously.*

What's the matter?

HEDDA. My piano doesn't go with these things.

TESMAN. We'll change it when my salary comes through.

HEDDA. I don't want to get rid of it, I want to put it there (*Points to the back.*) and get another one here. When we can, of course.

TESMAN. Yes. We could.

She picks up the flowers on the piano and looks at them.

I expect Aunt Juju brought them for you.

She takes a card from the flowers and reads it.

HEDDA. 'I'll come later in the day.' Guess who it's from?

TESMAN. No idea.

HEDDA. Guess.

TESMAN. Who is it?

HEDDA (*reading*). 'Mrs Elvsted.'

TESMAN. No! Mrs Elvsted?

HEDDA. Yes, Mrs Elvsted.

TESMAN. She used to be called Rysing.

HEDDA. Oh, I know Miss Rysing. Always showing off her golden curls. An old flame of yours.

TESMAN (*laughing*). Before I knew you, Hedda. For five minutes.

HEDDA. I only knew her at school. Why would she come to see us?

TESMAN. Perhaps because she can't bear being stuck in the provinces in that little northern town. I haven't seen her for ages.

HEDDA (*thinks for a moment*). Didn't he go there? Eilert Loevborg?

TESMAN. He did. Exactly.

BERTHE *comes in without knocking.*

BERTHE. She's here again, Madam. The lady who come by and left them flowers.

HEDDA. Is she? Well, show her in.

BERTHE *turns as* THEA ELVSTED *comes in. She's a lively woman, a couple of years younger than* HEDDA, *with a soft, attractive face. Blue eyes, blonde, almost golden hair – and lots of it. She's smartly but not fashionably dressed.*

Mrs Elvsted. How lovely to see you again.

THEA (*nervously*). And you. It's been such a long time.

TESMAN (*shaking hands*). For me as well, no?

HEDDA. Thank you for the flowers, they were –

THEA. Oh, please don't m . . . I'd have come when I arrived yesterday but I heard you were still away and . . .

TESMAN. Have you just come to town?

THEA. Lunchtime yesterday. I felt desperate when I heard you weren't at home.

HEDDA. Desperate?

TESMAN. Miss Ry . . . I mean Mrs Elvsted . . .

HEDDA. What's the matter?

THEA. I didn't know anyone here I could go to . . .

HEDDA *puts the flowers she's been holding on the table and goes to her.*

HEDDA. Sit . . .

THEA. I couldn't, I'm too . . .

HEDDA. Sit . . . let's sit here.

She draws THEA *down to the sofa and sits beside her.*

TESMAN. What is it?

HEDDA. Is it something at home?

THEA. It is and it isn't – I'm sorry, I'm not making sense . . .

HEDDA. Why don't you just tell us, Mrs Elvsted?

TESMAN. That's why you've come, no?

THEA. Yes . . . yes, it is. Well, you probably know that Eilert Loevborg is here and –

HEDDA. Here?

TESMAN. Eilert Loevborg in town? Amazing! Hedda, did you –

HEDDA. I heard.

THEA. He's been here a whole week. By himself. With every opportunity available . . .

HEDDA. But why does it matter to you?

THEA (*with a quick frightened glance*). He was my children's tutor.

HEDDA. Your children?

THEA. My husband's. I don't have children.

HEDDA. So your step-children.

THEA *nods.*

TESMAN (*cautiously*). Wasn't he too . . . um dissolute – I'm sorry, I mean was he *fit* enough to cope with working as a tutor?

THEA. There's been nothing that you could reproach him with for two years –

TESMAN. *Really*? Amazing! Hedda, do you –

HEDDA. I heard.

THEA. His reputation's been spotless, but here, where there's so much . . . well, temptation and he's got money and . . . well, I'm afraid for him.

TESMAN. Why couldn't he stay where he was? With you and your husband. No?

THEA. He couldn't settle after his book came out.

TESMAN. I've just heard about the new one.

THEA. It's a really big book, a sort of survey of cultural history. It came out about a fortnight ago and it's sold terribly well and been terribly well received –

TESMAN. I suppose it was something he had in a drawer.

THEA. From before, you mean?

TESMAN. Well . . . yes.

THEA (*shakes her head*). He wrote it when he was living with us. Over the whole of last year.

TESMAN. That's wonderful! Amazing, don't you think, Hedda?

HEDDA *doesn't respond.*

THEA. I just hope it'll last.

HEDDA. Have you seen him here?

THEA. Not yet. I didn't have his address until this morning.

HEDDA. Isn't it, well, a little *odd* for your husband –

THEA. What? What is?

HEDDA. For your husband to send you on a mission to keep an eye on his friend?

THEA. No no, he hasn't the time for that. He . . . I needed to do some shopping.

HEDDA (*smiling*). Well, why not?

THEA *gets up impulsively.*

THEA. Please, Mr Tesman . . . please give Eilert a warm
welcome if he comes to see you, I'm sure he will, you were
such good friends, and the work you do is so close to his
field, I mean, I think . . .

TESMAN. Well, it used to be, certainly.

THEA. And please do, *please* look after him, keep an eye on
him, will you? Please?

TESMAN. Of course I will Mrs, um, Rysing –

THEA. Elvsted.

TESMAN. I'll do whatever I can for him, anything.

THEA (*taking his hand between hers*). Thank you, thank you,
thank you. (*Murmuring.*) My husband's, well, he . . . he
thinks the world of him.

HEDDA *stands.*

HEDDA. You'll have to write to him, Tesman, he might not
come here without an invitation.

TESMAN. Yes. Right. Yes, Hedda. No?

HEDDA. Now.

THEA. Oh do, please . . .

TESMAN. I will. Right now. You have his address, Mrs, er . . .
Elvsted?

THEA (*handing him a piece of paper*). Here.

TESMAN. Fine. I'll . . . (*Looks around.*) Where are . . . ?
Right. Slippers . . . Ah *here* they are.

HEDDA. Write him a proper letter. Friendly.

TESMAN. Yes, of course.

THEA. You won't say anything about me asking?

TESMAN. I wouldn't dream of it, no?

He goes out through the back room.

HEDDA (*smiling*). Two birds with one stone.

THEA. What?

HEDDA. We've got him out of the way –

THEA. To write the letter?

HEDDA. To talk.

THEA (*confused*). About . . . ? About what?

HEDDA. About Eilert.

THEA. There's nothing to say.

HEDDA. Yes there is. There's a lot. Let's sit here.

She sits THEA *down in an armchair by the stove and pulls a stool close to her.*

THEA (*looking at her watch*). I've really got to go.

HEDDA. There's no hurry, you can tell me about home.

THEA. I really don't want to –

HEDDA. It's me, it's *me*. God, we went to school together.

THEA. You were two years above me and I was terrified of you.

HEDDA. Really?

THEA. You used to pull my hair if I passed you on the stairs.

HEDDA. Did I?

THEA. You said you'd set fire to it.

HEDDA. It was a joke.

THEA. Well, I took it seriously. Silly, I know. Anyway, we've not been close, stayed close and you were always, well, in a different world from me, socially, I mean.

HEDDA. We called each other by our Christian names at school –

THEA. We didn't.

HEDDA. We did, and now we will again.

HEDDA *moves close to* THEA *and kisses her cheek.*

You must call me Hedda and we'll swap secrets . . .

THEA (*holding* HEDDA'*s hand*). You're so kind, I'm not used to it . . .

HEDDA. . . . and I'll call you little Thora.

THEA. It's Thea.

HEDDA. Didn't I say Thea? (*Sympathetically.*) You haven't been much loved, Thea, have you? At home?

THEA. I've never had a home.

HEDDA. I thought not.

THEA (*helplessly*). Never . . . never . . . never . . .

HEDDA. You went as his housekeeper to Mr Elvsted's, didn't you?

THEA. Governess actually, but his wife was very ill, so I had to look after the house.

HEDDA. And then you became its mistress.

THEA (*heavily*). I did.

HEDDA. Three years ago?

THEA. Five. Oh God, those five years, the last two or three, Mrs Tesman –

HEDDA (*tapping her hand*). Hedda.

THEA. Oh Hedda, if you knew what it was like –

HEDDA (*casually*). Wasn't Eilert there for the last three years or so?

THEA. Eilert Loevborg? Yes. Yes, he was.

HEDDA. Had you known him here?

THEA. Barely. I knew him by name.

HEDDA. And he visited you up there?

THEA. He taught the children. We needed a tutor, I couldn't manage everything and . . .

HEDDA. Of course not, and your husband must have had to be away a lot . . .

THEA. He's the High Sheriff, so he has to travel all over and . . .

THEA *stops and* HEDDA *leans in to her.*

HEDDA. You must tell me everything, Thea.

THEA. What do you want to know?

HEDDA. What's your husband like? Is he kind?

THEA. I think . . . he thinks he is.

HEDDA. He's twenty years older than you, isn't he?

HEDDA's question hangs in the air.

THEA. We've got nothing in common. Nothing! I just can't bear him.

HEDDA. Does he love you at all?

THEA. Oh, I don't know. I'm useful to him. I'm cheap labour.

HEDDA. Thea . . .

THEA. It's true. He doesn't care about anyone. Maybe the children. Maybe.

HEDDA. But what about Eilert?

THEA. What about Eilert?

HEDDA. Well, you said to my husband, well, you *implied* that you'd been sent here to look after him.

THEA. Did I?

A silence.

My husband didn't know I was coming here.

HEDDA. *Really*?

THEA. How could he? He wasn't there. I just couldn't bear it any longer, I would have been alone there, for ever.

HEDDA. So?

THEA. So I packed a few things and I left the house.

HEDDA. Without a word to anyone?

THEA. I just caught the train here.

HEDDA. Thea, how brave.

THEA *stands.*

THEA. There was nothing else I could do!

HEDDA. What's your husband going to say when he gets back?

THEA. Back home?

HEDDA. Well . . . yes.

THEA. I won't go back.

HEDDA (*rising*). So you've really, really, seriously, left him.

THEA. There wasn't anything else I could do.

HEDDA. You went in broad daylight?

THEA. How could I hide?

HEDDA. What will people say, Thea?

THEA. They can say whatever they like, for heaven's sake,
I did what I had to do.

She sits wearily. A silence.

HEDDA. What will you do now?

THEA. I don't know. I only know that if I'm to stay alive I have
to live where Eilert is living.

HEDDA *sits near* THEA.

HEDDA. How did this . . . relationship with Eilert start?

THEA. It just . . . happened. Bit by bit. I seemed to have some
sort of power over him.

HEDDA. Power?

THEA. He gave up his drinking and . . . his bad behaviour. I
didn't ask him to, I wouldn't have dared, he seemed to
know that I didn't like that sort of thing and so he . . . he
stopped.

HEDDA. So . . . (*She hides a small smile.*) . . . you've 'saved'
him, have you, little Thea?

THEA. That's what he says. And he's made me feel . . . that
I exist, that I'm really alive. He's taught me to think, to
understand things.

HEDDA. So he was your tutor as well.

THEA. He talked to me. About everything. And then one day
. . . one extraordinary day . . . he asked me to help him with
his work. Me.

HEDDA. So you helped him.

THEA. He wanted me to write with him.

HEDDA. As friends?

THEA. Yes, friends. We were 'collaborators'. That's what he
called us. I could be so happy now but I just don't know if
it'll last.

HEDDA. Why are you so unsure?

THEA (*sighing*). There's a . . . a . . . sort of ghost standing
between us.

HEDDA. Who?

THEA. A woman he can't forget.

HEDDA. Has he said anything about her?

THEA. Once.

HEDDA. What did he say?

THEA (*slowly*). He said that when they parted she threatened
to shoot him.

HEDDA. People don't do things like that.

THEA. He knew a . . . well, I think she was a . . . a p . . . a
performer, a dancer or a singer. She had red hair . . .

HEDDA. Could be . . .

THEA. She went around with a loaded revolver in her –

HEDDA. Must be her.

THEA. I've heard that she's here. I can't bear it, Hedda –

HEDDA. Ssshhh! Tesman's coming.

She gets up, puts her fingers to THEA*'s lips.*

This is between us.

THEA. Oh Lord, yes, please.

TESMAN *comes in through the back room.*

TESMAN. The missive is signed and sealed.

HEDDA. Mrs Elvsted is about to go. (*To* THEA.) I'll walk you
to the door.

TESMAN. Could Berthe take the . . .

HEDDA (*taking the letter from him*). I'll tell her.

BERTHE *comes in from the hall.*

Oh Berthe, take this letter to the post.

BERTHE. His Honour Judge Brack's here. Says he'd like to pay his respects to the Doctor and his lady wife.

HEDDA. Well ask 'his Honour' to come in. And don't forget the letter.

BERTHE (*taking the letter*). Yes ma'am.

She shows JUDGE BRACK *in and goes.* BRACK *is 45-ish, stocky but fit; a round face, short dark hair and moustache. He wears a fashionable grey suit, perhaps too young for him. He uses a monocle; a dapper upper-middle-class man.*

BRACK (*holding out his hand to* HEDDA). May I presume that I'm not too early in the day?

HEDDA. You may presume.

TESMAN (*shaking hands*). We'll always be pleased to see you. Do you know each other? Judge Brack, Miss Rysing, er . . .

HEDDA *sighs heavily in irritation.*

BRACK (*bows to* THEA). *Enchanté.*

HEDDA. It's a delight to see you by daylight, 'your Honour'.

BRACK. Am I different?

HEDDA. Younger perhaps.

BRACK. You're very kind.

TESMAN. What of Hedda? Isn't she blossoming –

HEDDA. Don't. Why don't you occupy yourself with thanking Judge Brack for all the trouble he's gone to?

BRACK. Rubbish, it was a joy.

HEDDA. You're a saint. Will you excuse me, your Honour, my friend's eager to leave. I'll be back.

After goodbyes between THEA *and the others, she leaves with* HEDDA.

BRACK. Well, is your wife now content?

TESMAN. We can't thank you enough. Perfect. Apart from the odd shift of furniture and a few more things to buy.

BRACK. Oh really?

TESMAN. Please don't bother yourself, Hedda said she'd um . . . Shall we sit? No?

BRACK (*sitting*). Thank you. There's something that I think we should talk about.

TESMAN (*sitting*). After the pleasure, the payment, no?

BRACK. There's no urgency about the money, even if I do wish everything were a little less grand.

TESMAN. Absolutely not possible. This is Hedda, you know her well, I couldn't possibly have asked her to live in a little suburban rabbit hutch.

BRACK. No, it's a problem . . .

TESMAN. But it won't be when I get my professorship.

BRACK. These things can take time.

TESMAN. You've heard something, no?

BRACK. No . . . I do have one bit of news.

TESMAN. Yes?

BRACK. Your chum Eilert Loevborg is back.

TESMAN. Mrs Elvsted told me.

BRACK. Mrs Elvsted?

TESMAN. She was just here . . .

BRACK. Mrs Elvsted indeed. The High Sheriff's wife. Loevborg's been staying at their house.

TESMAN. And I'm thrilled to hear that he's completely reformed.

BRACK. So they say.

TESMAN. And has a new book out.

BRACK. He has.

TESMAN. Which has made a bit of a splash.

BRACK. A splash, certainly.

TESMAN. Well, that's wonderful. He's so talented and I thought he was sunk for ever.

BRACK. Yes, most people did.

TESMAN. But what's he going to do now? What'll he live on? No?

She comes back into the room.

HEDDA. Tesman is always worrying about how people earn a crust. (*Sharply, mimicking him.*) No?

TESMAN (*taken by surprise*). Hedda! We were talking about the troubles of Eilert Loevborg.

HEDDA. Were you? And what is his trouble?

TESMAN. Well, he must have got through the money he was left long ago, and he can't produce a new book every year, no? So I'm just speculating about what will happen to him.

BRACK. Let me add to your speculation.

TESMAN. What?

BRACK. You know he has influential relatives . . .

TESMAN. Who have washed their hands of him.

BRACK. Who used to regard him as the golden boy . . .

TESMAN. Not any more.

HEDDA. How do you know? After all, he's been 'saved', hasn't he, at the High Sheriff's house . . .

BRACK. . . . and written a new book.

TESMAN. Well, good luck to him. I've just written to ask him to dinner here this evening.

BRACK. You're supposed to be having dinner with me tonight. Men only. You agreed to it last night.

HEDDA. You'd forgotten, hadn't you?

TESMAN (*shaking his head*). I had.

BRACK. Loevborg won't come, of course.

TESMAN. Why not?

BRACK *gets up, leans on the back of a chair.*

BRACK. I'd better tell you something – both of you.

TESMAN. About Eilert?

BRACK. And you.

TESMAN (*puzzled*). What?

BRACK. Your professorship . . . might not come through quite as punctually as you expect.

TESMAN (*jumping up*). What!

BRACK. The appointment may be opened up to other applicants.

TESMAN. Really?

HEDDA (*to herself*). Oh, I see . . . I *see* . . .

TESMAN. You don't mean Eilert Loevborg?

BRACK. I do.

TESMAN. That's – well, it's unthinkable, it's impossible, I –

BRACK. Impossible but probable.

TESMAN. But it would be so incredibly inconsiderate to me. I've just got married. We got married on the prospect of the job and we've got debts, and I've borrowed Aunt Juju's money. God, I was as good as *promised* that professorship.

BRACK. *Calmez-vous, mon vieux, soyez tranquil.* I'm sure you'll get the job, there'll just be a little competition for it.

HEDDA (*very still*). It'll be like a duel.

TESMAN (*to* HEDDA). How can you be so cool about it?

HEDDA. I'm not, I'm trembling for the outcome.

BRACK. Whatever the outcome, I thought you should know how things stand . . . (*To* HEDDA.) I mean, before you make any extravagant plans for the house.

HEDDA. It won't make any difference to my plans.

BRACK. Well, that's your business, I suppose. (*To* TESMAN.) I'll come in and fetch you this evening.

TESMAN. Oh yes . . . yes . . . I don't know what I'm . . .

HEDDA *leans back and holds out her hand to* BRACK.

HEDDA. Au revoir, your Honour. I'll see you later.

BRACK *takes her hand and then goes out.* TESMAN *paces restlessly.*

TESMAN. One should never try to live out a fantasy.

HEDDA (*smiles*). Is that what you've done?

TESMAN. We got married and bought the house on my hopes of the . . . (*He shrugs.*) It was a fantasy.

HEDDA. Perhaps.

TESMAN. But at least we've got the house, the paradise we dreamed about, no?

HEDDA. We agreed we'd live in a certain style.

TESMAN. Don't think I didn't look forward to that. With your . . . your salon, and you . . . glowing at the centre of it. Well, we'll, for now, we'll just have each other and see Aunt Juju of course, but . . . oh God, Hedda, it shouldn't have been like this.

HEDDA *rises wearily.*

HEDDA. So no butler . . .

TESMAN. Butler?

HEDDA. And no horse . . .

TESMAN. Horse!

HEDDA. But I do at least have one thing to cheer me up.

TESMAN (*smiling*). I'm so glad. What? What is it, Hedda?

At the opening to the back room.

HEDDA. My guns . . . George.

TESMAN. What?

HEDDA. My father's guns. General Gabler's pistols.

She goes out. TESMAN *follows.*

TESMAN. Please Hedda, please don't get them out. Hedda!

Fade to black.

ACT TWO

It's early evening on the same day. Golden autumn light.

The room has been changed: the piano has been moved into the back room and a desk has replaced it. Most of the flowers have gone but THEA's *bouquet is now in a vase in the centre of the table.*

HEDDA *is alone. She's dressed now for receiving visitors, standing by the open French windows, putting a bullet in a pistol.*

HEDDA. Hello again, your Honour!

BRACK (*from the garden*). Hello, Mrs Tesman!

    HEDDA *raises the pistol and carefully takes aim.*

HEDDA. I'm going to shoot you, your Honour –

BRACK. Don't point it at me! Don't ever p –

HEDDA. This is what you get for not coming in the front door.

    She fires.

BRACK. ARE YOU INSANE!

HEDDA. Oh no, did I hit you?

BRACK. Stop this, NOW!

HEDDA. Then come in . . .

    He does so, shaking with anger.

Your Honour.

    BRACK *is dressed for his dinner party in dinner jacket, carrying a light overcoat over his arm.*

BRACK. What the hell do you think you're doing! What the hell are you shooting at!

HEDDA. The sky.

BRACK. Give it to me. (*Taking the pistol gently from her hand.*) It looks only too familiar. Where's the case?

He sees the case and puts the pistol into it.

Enough games for today, I think.

HEDDA. Why, what else do I have to do?

BRACK. Haven't you had any visitors?

She shuts the French windows.

HEDDA. Everyone must still be in the country.

BRACK. And your husband?

HEDDA *locks the pistols in a drawer.*

HEDDA. He ran off to his auntie as soon as he'd had lunch. He was expecting you later.

BRACK. Careless of me.

HEDDA. What?

BRACK. I should have come earlier.

HEDDA. I was in my bedroom, dressing.

BRACK. And there's not a tiny crack in the door, I suppose. For me to speak to you.

HEDDA. You forgot to arrange one.

BRACK. Careless of me.

HEDDA. My husband won't be home for some time. You'll just have to be patient.

BRACK. Shame, I'll just have to be patient.

HEDDA *sits on the sofa, leaving room for* BRACK, *who sits on a chair. He puts his coat over the arm of the sofa and keeps his hat on his knee. A pause. They look at each other.*

HEDDA. So?

BRACK (*imitating her*). So?

HEDDA. I asked first.

BRACK. So let's have a chat, Mrs Tesman.

HEDDA. It feels a lifetime since we last talked. I don't count last night or this morning.

BRACK. You mean talked *à deux*.

HEDDA. *A deux*, yes.

BRACK. I've come here every day, wishing that you were here.

HEDDA. And all the time I was away . . . I was wishing the same thing.

BRACK (*slowly*). Mrs . . . Tesman. Are you telling the truth? I thought that you were loving your wonderful honeymoon.

HEDDA. Loving it.

BRACK. That's what your husband said in his letters. 'Wonderful,' he said.

HEDDA. He thinks it's wonderful to burrow around in libraries and copy out old documents, or whatever it is he does with them.

BRACK. Well, it's more or less what he was put on earth to do.

HEDDA. But I wasn't and I was bored, bored, bored.

BRACK. Really? Honestly?

HEDDA. Can you imagine spending six months and not meeting a single person of your class? Not one person you can talk to?

BRACK. Yes, I would find that an ordeal.

HEDDA. But the most unbearable thing . . .

BRACK. Yes?

HEDDA. *The* most unbearable . . . is to have to spend every minute of every day with –

BRACK. With the same person. Morning, noon –

HEDDA. And night. Yes.

BRACK. But Tesman is an . . . he's decent, he's, well . . .

HEDDA. He's an academic.

BRACK. Indeed.

HEDDA. And academics are not very good company.

BRACK. Even academics one loves.

HEDDA. Oh, don't be so sentimental.

BRACK. Mrs Hedda . . .

HEDDA. You should try it. Nothing but early, middle and late medieval handicrafts.

BRACK. For the rest of recorded time.

HEDDA. Yes! All that stuff about domestic crafts, it's so *tedious*!

BRACK. Well, how did . . . I mean, why . . . ?

HEDDA. . . . did Tesman and I marry?

BRACK. Well, yes.

HEDDA. Is it so bizarre?

BRACK. Yes. And no.

HEDDA. It was time to leave the dance floor – (*Shudders.*) Oh God, I don't want to think about it.

BRACK. You've no reason to think . . .

HEDDA. Oh . . . *reason* . . .

She looks at him questioningly.

Isn't George Tesman a thoroughly respectable and dependable man?

BRACK. Respectable and dependable, yes.

HEDDA. Not ridiculous?

BRACK. Not entirely . . .

HEDDA. A diligent researcher who will climb the ladder rung by rung . . .

BRACK. You don't share the widespread opinion that he's a high-flyer?

She looks weary with the interrogation.

HEDDA. Oh, I did, I did . . . and when he made such a fuss of me, of wanting to be allowed to provide for me, I, well, why wouldn't I let him?

BRACK. If you look at it from that angle . . .

HEDDA. Is there another? It was more than my other admirers were prepared to do.

BRACK (*laughing*). I can't answer for them. I've always rather
. . . yearned for the institution of marriage. In theory.

HEDDA. Oh, I never had any hopes of you.

BRACK. All I want in the world . . . is to be an important part
of the lives . . . of people who I help and advise . . . and the
freedom to come and go as . . . a friend who can be trusted.

HEDDA. A friend of the husband?

BRACK *leans towards* HEDDA.

BRACK. I'd rather it was the wife, to be honest. You know that
sort of . . . domestic triangle, one might call it . . . can be,
well, a pleasure for all parties.

HEDDA. I used to long for a third person when I was trapped
in those railway compartments on the honeymoon.

BRACK. Well, the honeymoon's over now.

HEDDA. I've only stopped at a station.

BRACK. Why not jump off and stretch your legs?

HEDDA. No, I won't jump.

BRACK. Really?

HEDDA. No, there'll always be someone who's . . .

BRACK. Watching your step?

HEDDA. Yes.

BRACK. But, dear God, Hedda –

HEDDA. No, I couldn't do it. I'd rather accept where I am
now, stuck in the compartment, just the two of us.

A pause.

BRACK. And what if another man stepped into the
compartment . . .

HEDDA. Ah well . . .

BRACK. A sympathetic friend . . .

HEDDA. Who could be amusing about all sorts of things . . . ?

BRACK. Without an atom of the academic about him . . . ?

HEDDA (*sighing*). Well, that would be different.

The sound of the front door opening.

BRACK (*nodding toward the door*). The triangle's complete.

HEDDA (*murmurs*). And the train rolls on.

TESMAN, *wearing a grey suit and a soft felt hat comes in from the hall. He has books under his arm and journals stuffed in his pockets. He puts the books down on a table.*

TESMAN. Ooof . . . I'm pouring sweat, Hedda. It was boiling humping these up here. (*Noticing* BRACK.) Oh, you're here already, no? Berthe didn't mention that you'd come.

BRACK (*standing*). I came through the garden.

HEDDA. What on earth are those?

TESMAN. Books and journals. They're just published.

HEDDA. Academic journals?

BRACK (*smiling at her*). Academic, Mrs Tesman.

HEDDA. Don't you have enough of them?

TESMAN. One has to keep up with the latest research.

HEDDA. Does one?

TESMAN (*sorting through his books*). Look, I've bought Eilert's book too. You'd like to look at it, no?

HEDDA. No. Thank you. Later perhaps.

TESMAN. I had a peep on the way back.

BRACK. And what did you think? As an academic?

TESMAN. Clear-headed. Thoughtful. He didn't write like that before. Extraordinary.

TESMAN *gathers up his books and journals.*

I can't wait to read these. I must change. *(To* BRACK.) We don't need to leave now, no?

BRACK. No. No hurry.

TESMAN. I'll take my time, then.

He starts to leave the room and then stops and turns to HEDDA.

Oh Hedda, Aunt Juju won't be coming to see you this evening.

HEDDA. Is it the hat?

TESMAN. How could you think that of her? It's Auntie Rena. She's very ill.

HEDDA. She's always ill.

TESMAN. She was in such a bad way today.

HEDDA. Then I'm sure it's right that the well one stays to look after the ill one. I'll just have to bear the solitude.

TESMAN. She was so thrilled about how you've filled out since we've been away.

HEDDA (*hissing*). These perpetual . . . *aunts*.

TESMAN. What?

HEDDA. Nothing.

TESMAN. Right.

TESMAN *goes out through the back room.*

BRACK. What hat?

HEDDA. Oh, his aunt left her hat on the chair this morning and . . . (*She smiles at him.*) I pretended I thought it was the maid's.

BRACK. Hedda, how could you? That sweet old lady.

HEDDA (*pacing restlessly*). I couldn't help myself. I get these feelings and – I don't know why, I just can't stop.

She throws herself into the armchair.

I don't know why I do it.

BRACK (*behind the chair*). You're unhappy.

HEDDA. Why should I be happy?

BRACK. Well, among other things, you've got exactly the house you wanted.

HEDDA. Oh, you don't believe in that 'fantasy' rubbish, do you?

BRACK. Was it rubbish?

HEDDA. God, yes. Mostly.

BRACK. Mostly.

HEDDA. Well . . . I used to let Tesman walk me home from dances last summer . . .

BRACK. When sadly I was walking in another direction . . .

HEDDA. Indeed you were.

BRACK. You're shameless, Madame Hedda. So . . . you and Tesman . . .

HEDDA. . . . were walking past this house and the poor creature was contorting himself in agony because he didn't have an idea what to say to me . . . and I felt sorry for the learned man . . .

BRACK. Sounds improbable . . .

HEDDA. I *did*! So to . . . help him out of his misery I pretended – for fun – that I'd love to live in this house.

BRACK. And that was it.

HEDDA. Then.

BRACK. And after?

HEDDA. My game had a consequence, your Honour.

BRACK. Games usually do, Mrs Tesman.

HEDDA. Thank you. We found that we shared, we shared an enthusiasm . . . for the house of the widow of the Cabinet Minister. And that . . . enthusiasm led to our engagement and our wedding and our honeymoon and . . . yes, well, as you make your bed so you must lie in it, you might say.

BRACK. You didn't really give a damn about this house!

HEDDA. Heavens, not a bit.

BRACK. What about now? Now that it's been done up so beautifully for you?

HEDDA. Eeeugh, I can't stand the smell of lavender and roses everywhere. But maybe that's 'Aunt Juju'.

BRACK (*laughs*). I rather think it's the legacy of the late widow of the late Minister.

HEDDA. Well, there's something dead about it. It reminds me of flowers the day after a dance.

She folds her hands behind her head, leans back, stretching her legs, and looks up at BRACK.

You can't imagine how bored I'm going to be here.

BRACK. Is there nothing in life to absorb you?

HEDDA. You mean a challenge?

BRACK. Preferably.

HEDDA. God knows what that could be. Although I've often thought – but that's pointless too.

BRACK. What? Tell me.

HEDDA. I've often thought that I should get Tesman to go into politics.

BRACK (*laughing*). Tesman! Tesman in politics! It's ridiculous!

HEDDA. Well, maybe it is, but what if I could persuade him –

BRACK. What possible joy could there be in that? He'd be out of his depth and . . . why waste your time with that?

HEDDA. Because I'm BORED!

A pause.

(*Straight-faced.*) You think it would be totally impossible for Tesman to become Prime Minister?

BRACK. Prime Minster? Ha . . . well, for that he'd have to have money.

HEDDA (*getting up*). Well, we don't have any money! That's what makes my life so miserable and ridiculous. Well, it *is*!

BRACK. I think there's another reason.

HEDDA. What?

BRACK. You've never really been engaged by anything, have you?

HEDDA. You mean anything serious?

BRACK. Well, that as well, but now that –

HEDDA. Oh God – that nonsense about the professor thing. That's his business, it's nothing to do with me.

BRACK. No, possibly not, but suppose something happened . . . (*Smiling.*) Something serious that made . . . grown-up demands on you – ?

HEDDA. Oh shut up! It won't happen!

BRACK. Well . . . let's see in a year's time. Or even earlier.

HEDDA. I don't want that sort of responsibility. It's out of the question.

BRACK. Don't you feel, as a woman . . . I mean, that it's your vocation to –

HEDDA. Shut *up*, will you!

She moves to the French windows and stands staring out.

There's only one thing I have a vocation for.

BRACK (*quietly, coming near her*). And what's that?

HEDDA. Boring myself to death. Now you know.

She turns and, as she does so, sees TESMAN *coming through the back room.*

And talking of boring, here comes the Professor.

BRACK. Now, now, Mrs Tesman . . .

TESMAN *is dressed for the party: dinner jacket, hat and gloves.*

TESMAN. There's no message from Eilert, Hedda, no?

HEDDA. No.

TESMAN. Then he'll be here soon.

BRACK. You're sure he'll come?

TESMAN. Almost – it's just gossip, that stuff you were telling us about this morning.

BRACK. Really?

TESMAN. Aunt Juju said that he'd never dare to block my promotion. (*Shaking his head.*) Amazing.

BRACK. Well . . . fine.

TESMAN. Yes, so you must let me wait for him.

BRACK. No one's arriving at my house till seven . . . half past seven at the earliest.

TESMAN. Then we can keep Hedda company and see if he arrives, no?

HEDDA. And if there's a disaster, Mr Loevborg can come and sit here with me.

HEDDA *goes to the sofa where she picks up* BRACK*'s hat and coat.* BRACK *intercepts her, offering to take them from her.*

BRACK. Let me. What do you mean, 'if there's a disaster'?

HEDDA. I mean if he doesn't want to go with you and Tesman.

TESMAN. Hedda, would it . . . do you think it would be right for him to stay here with you, no? I mean without Aunt Juju?

HEDDA. But *with* Mrs Elvsted.

TESMAN. Oh.

HEDDA. We'll all have a cup of tea, Tesman.

TESMAN. Oh, fine. That'll be fine.

BRACK (*smiling*). And probably the safest solution for him.

HEDDA. Why?

BRACK. Good God, Mrs Tesman, you always say my gatherings are only suitable for men of iron discipline.

HEDDA. But surely Mr Loevborg is sufficiently disciplined now. You know what they say about converts –

BERTHE *comes in from the hall.*

BERTHE. There's a gentleman here, ma'am, wants to come in –

HEDDA. Well, let him come.

TESMAN (*slowly*). It must be him. Amazing.

EILERT LOEVBORG *comes in from the hall. He's about the same age as* TESMAN, *but looks older: good looking, thin, gaunt and somewhat wasted.*

LOEVBORG's hair and beard are dark brown; he has some red blotches on his cheeks. He's dressed fashionably in a fairly new suit, top hat, an overcoat in the pocket of which is a bulky envelope. He stops near the door and bows briskly. He seems embarrassed. When he speaks, his voice is quiet.

Eilert!

LOEVBORG. Thank you for your note. (*Offering his hand to* HEDDA). Mrs Tesman.

HEDDA. Mr Loevborg. Do you two . . . ?

LOEVBORG. It's Judge Brack, isn't it?

BRACK. It is. It's, um, been a while . . .

TESMAN (*with a hand on* LOEVBORG's *shoulder*). You must make yourself at home here, Eilert. Mustn't he, Hedda? I hear you're moving back here, no?

LOEVBORG. I am.

TESMAN. Excellent. Listen – I just got your book but I haven't had a chance to read it yet.

LOEVBORG. I shouldn't bother.

TESMAN. What?

LOEVBORG. There's nothing in it.

TESMAN (*shaking his head*). Amazing.

BRACK. It's been highly praised.

LOEVBORG. I wanted it to be popular, so I wrote it with an ingratiating smile on its face.

BRACK. Very shrewd.

TESMAN. Why?

LOEVBORG. I wanted to make myself acceptable.

TESMAN. Oh yes. Yes, of course, I can see that.

LOEVBORG smiles at TESMAN *and pulls a manuscript in an envelope from his overcoat pocket.*

LOEVBORG. But you're going to have to read this one when it comes out, George. This one is the genuine one: this is my real voice.

TESMAN. What does it say?

LOEVBORG. It carries on.

TESMAN. From . . . what?

LOEVBORG. From the new one.

TESMAN. The one you've just published?

LOEVBORG. Of course.

TESMAN. But . . . that goes up to the present day.

LOEVBORG. Yes and this one goes into the future.

TESMAN. Lord – the future! We don't know anything about it.

LOEVBORG. But that doesn't stop us speaking about it.

He opens the envelope.

Look –

TESMAN. That's not your writing.

LOEVBORG. I dictated it. Look – it's in two parts. The first's about the power of art in our society and the second's about the way in which society could develop.

TESMAN. Amazing! I'd never think of writing something like that.

HEDDA *is by the window, drumming her fingers on the panes.*

HEDDA. Well . . . no.

LOEVBORG *puts the manuscript back in the envelope and puts the envelope on the table.*

LOEVBORG. I thought I might read some of it to you this evening.

TESMAN. That's very kind but . . . (*Looking at* BRACK.) . . . I'm, er, not sure how –

LOEVBORG. Oh, there's no hurry, another time.

BRACK. I'm having a dinner at my house tonight in Tesman's honour.

LOEVBORG. Oh, well then, I won't –

He picks up the envelope and looks for his hat.

BRACK. No, why don't you join us?

LOEVBORG (*sharply*). No! No. Thank you.

BRACK. Oh, come on. It's only a small dinner for friends. You can be sure the evening will be a 'merry' one, as Hed – Mrs Tesman would say.

LOEVBORG. I'm sure but –

BRACK. You could read your manuscript to Tesman at my house.

TESMAN. That's what you should do, Eilert, no?

HEDDA *walks between them.*

HEDDA. But he doesn't *want* to, Tesman dear. I'm sure Mr Loevborg would rather stay here for supper.

LOEVBORG. With you?

HEDDA. And Mrs Elvsted.

LOEVBORG. Oh, Mrs Elvsted. I, um, ran into her this afternoon.

HEDDA. Really? Well, she's coming here, so you have to stay. Otherwise there'll be no one to see her home.

LOEVBORG. No. Well, thank you, Mrs . . . er . . . I'll be happy to stay.

HEDDA. I'll tell the maid.

HEDDA *rings for* BERTHE, *who comes in.* HEDDA *whispers instructions, pointing to the back room;* BERTHE *nods and goes out. Meanwhile* TESMAN *continues.*

TESMAN. Eilert, are you . . . this new thesis, the stuff about the future and everything . . . are you planning to lecture on it?

LOEVBORG. Yes, I am.

TESMAN. They said in the bookshop that you were planning to give some lectures in the autumn.

LOEVBORG. Yes, I'd like to. Is there something wrong with that?

TESMAN. Lord, no, it's just –

LOEVBORG. I can understand it might be infuriating for you.

TESMAN. Well, I can hardly ask you to –

LOEVBORG. I'll wait until you've been appointed.

TESMAN. You'll wait? But, don't you . . . don't you want to compete for the job, no?

LOEVBORG. You take the professorship, I'd rather have fame.

TESMAN. But, good Lord, you mean – so Aunt Juju was right, Hedda, Eilert doesn't want to stand in our way.

HEDDA. *Your* way. Leave me out of it.

She goes to the back room where BERTHE *is putting glasses and a jug on the table, nods to her, and returns.* TESMAN *continues.*

TESMAN. What do you think, Judge Brack? You heard, no?

BRACK. Oh, I think fame – in whatever form – can be very alluring.

TESMAN. Yes, of course it can, but –

HEDDA (*to* TESMAN). You look as if you've been struck by lightning.

TESMAN. I . . . more or less . . .

BRACK. There were dark clouds overhead. But now they've passed.

HEDDA. Would you men like to have a glass to refresh you? Cold punch.

BRACK (*looking at his watch*). A snifter before we go? Why not.

TESMAN. Wonderful idea, Hedda. Marvellous. I feel light-headed.

HEDDA. Mr Loevborg?

LOEVBORG (*curtly*). No! Not for me, thank you.

BRACK. Good God, man, it's only punch, it's not poisonous.

LOEVBORG. Not for you.

HEDDA. I'll entertain Mr Loevborg.

TESMAN. Good idea, Hedda.

BRACK *and* TESMAN *go into the back room where they drink and smoke.* LOEVBORG *stands by the stove;* HEDDA *moves to the desk, where she picks up an album of photographs.*

HEDDA (*slightly louder than necessary*). I'll show you some photographs of our honeymoon. In the Tyrol.

She moves to the sofa and sits in the corner of it. LOEVBORG *looks at her for a moment, then takes a chair and sits near her with his back to the others. The sun is setting.* LOEVBORG *and* HEDDA *are in shadow. Dusk light falls over the room.* LOEVBORG *looks at her unwaveringly. She opens the album.*

Look at the mountains. They're called the Ortler Mountains. You see what Tesman's written underneath: 'The Ortler Mountains.'

LOEVBORG. Hedda . . . Gabler . . .

HEDDA. Sshhh . . .

LOEVBORG. Hedda . . . Gabler . . .

HEDDA. I was.

LOEVBORG. And I have to stop saying Hedda . . . Gabler.

HEDDA. Yes, you do. Now.

LOEVBORG. Hedda . . . Tesman.

HEDDA. Yes. That's how it is.

LOEVBORG. How could you?

HEDDA. Don't!

LOEVBORG. Don't what?

TESMAN comes into the room.

HEDDA. This is taken from the Ampezzo Valley. Look at those mountains. (*To* TESMAN.) What were they called?

TESMAN. Let's see. Oh, they're the Dolomites.

HEDDA. Of course. These are the Dolomites, Mr Loevborg.

TESMAN. I just wondered if you'd like a glass of punch, Hedda, no?

HEDDA. Thank you. And maybe some canapés.

TESMAN. Cigarette?

HEDDA. No.

TESMAN. Right.

He goes into the back room.

LOEVBORG. So, Hedda . . . darling . . . how could you?

HEDDA. If you go on calling me 'darling', I won't talk to you.

LOEVBORG. Even when we're alone?

HEDDA. You can think it, but don't say it.

LOEVBORG. Because you love George Tesman.

HEDDA. Love?

LOEVBORG. Not love?

HEDDA. But not . . . infidelity. I won't be unfaithful.

LOEVBORG. Hedda, just tell me one thing –

HEDDA. Ssshh!

TESMAN *comes from the back room with a tray – glasses, jug of punch, canapés.*

TESMAN. Here are the treats.

HEDDA. Why are you waiting on us?

TESMAN (*pouring the punch*). I like to serve you, Hedda.

HEDDA. Mr Loevborg doesn't want a glass.

TESMAN. But Mrs Elvsted'll be here soon.

HEDDA. Oh. Yes.

TESMAN. You'd forgotten, no?

HEDDA. We were so caught up in this. Do you remember this little village?

TESMAN. Oh, that's the one – it's at the foot of the Bremmer Pass – *that's* the one where we stayed, you remember, Hedda, that night we –

HEDDA (*to* LOEVBORG). We met some jolly tourists.

TESMAN (*laughing*). You should have been there, Eilert.

He goes to join BRACK.

LOEVBORG. Tell me one thing, Hedda . . .

HEDDA. What?

LOEVBORG. Did you love me? A spark? A flicker perhaps?

HEDDA *shakes her head, wondering.*

HEDDA. We were really good friends. We had no secrets. (*Smiles.*) And you told me everything.

LOEVBORG. You wanted to know everything.

HEDDA. And no one knew. It was . . . thrilling. Exciting. And brave.

LOEVBORG. It was, wasn't it? When I came to see your father in the afternoons and the General sat by the window with his back to us, reading the papers . . .

HEDDA. While we sat on the sofa in the corner . . .

LOEVBORG. . . . reading a magazine . . .

HEDDA. Always the same one, we didn't have an album.

LOEVBORG. I told you things about myself that no one knew. My drinking and the . . . days and nights of . . . dissipation. What was it in you that made me do that?

HEDDA. What was it?

LOEVBORG. Some . . . power you had, I don't know. All those questions you asked, never quite to the point.

HEDDA. Which you always understood.

LOEVBORG. How could you have been so bold?

HEDDA. I thought I was never to the point.

LOEVBORG. You asked about everything.

HEDDA. And you answered everything, Mr Loevborg.

LOEVBORG. Wasn't that love? When I confessed, didn't you want to absolve me, to wash me clean of my sins?

HEDDA. Not really.

LOEVBORG. Then what?

HEDDA. Do you really find it so difficult to understand that a young girl . . . in secret . . . could take the opportunity to . . .

LOEVBORG. What?

HEDDA. To look into a world that . . .

LOEVBORG. That?

HEDDA. That . . . A world she's not supposed to know anything about . . .

LOEVBORG. Was that all it was?

HEDDA. Partly. Mostly, I think.

LOEVBORG. If you didn't love me, then we were still friends, weren't we? Why couldn't that have lasted?

HEDDA. It was your fault.

LOEVBORG. You broke it off.

HEDDA. When it was threatening to become something else. Why did you try to force yourself on me? I was your friend, however bold I may have been.

LOEVBORG (*in agony*). Then why didn't you shoot me when you said you were going to?

HEDDA. I was afraid of scandal.

LOEVBORG. You're a coward.

HEDDA. Yes, I was a coward. Anyway, you found consolation at the Elvsteds.

LOEVBORG. I know what Thea's told you.

HEDDA. And have you told her about us?

LOEVBORG. She wouldn't understand, she's a fool.

HEDDA. A fool?

LOEVBORG. In that sort of thing she's a fool.

HEDDA. And I'm a coward.

There's a long uneasy silence. HEDDA *leans closer to him, without looking at him, and speaks very quietly.*

I want to tell you something.

LOEVBORG. What?

HEDDA. Not shooting you . . .

LOEVBORG. Yes?

HEDDA. Not having the courage to shoot you . . . wasn't . . . the most cowardly thing I did that night.

He looks at HEDDA *for a moment, hardly able to believe what he's hearing. Then he puts his hand on her knee, strokes the outside of her thigh and whispers to her.*

LOEVBORG. Oh Hedda . . . Hedda . . . Now I can see why you wanted to know all those things. You just longed to live, you wanted to really be alive –

HEDDA. Don't . . . That's enough!

He takes his hand away. There's a heavy silence, neither person moves. It's beginning to get dark. BERTHE *comes in from the hall and* HEDDA *snaps the album shut.*

Thea, darling, there you are!

THEA *comes in. She's dressed for the evening. She nods towards the men in the back room and goes to* HEDDA *who holds out her arms to her. She acknowledges* LOEVBORG *with a nod.*

My sweet Thea, I'm so glad to see you.

THEA. Should I go and chat to your husband?

HEDDA. Oh, let them be, they're going soon.

THEA. Going out?

HEDDA. Out on the town.

THEA (*to* LOEVBORG). You're not going?

LOEVBORG. No.

HEDDA. Mr Loevborg . . . will stay with us.

THEA. It's so nice to be here.

She takes a chair to sit next to LOEVBORG.

HEDDA. Oh no, don't sit there. Come and sit here – I'll be in the middle.

THEA. If you want.

THEA sits on the sofa next to HEDDA. *There's a pause.*

LOEVBORG. Isn't she lovely to look at?

HEDDA (*stroking* THEA's *hair*). Just to look at?

LOEVBORG. Yes. We're true friends who can sit together and talk honestly –

HEDDA. To the point, no doubt?

He's about to reply when THEA *takes* HEDDA's *arm.*

THEA. I'm so happy. Just think, Hedda, Eilert says I've inspired him.

HEDDA (*smiling*). Does he?

LOEVBORG. She has the courage of her convictions.

THEA. Courage? Me?

LOEVBORG. To fight for her friends.

HEDDA. Oh, if one only had that sort of courage.

LOEVBORG. What . . . ?

HEDDA. Then perhaps one could . . . really be alive. Thea, darling, have a glass of punch.

THEA. Oh, no thank you, I never drink alcohol.

HEDDA. Mr Loevborg?

She looks challengingly at LOEVBORG, *holding out a glass to him.*

LOEVBORG. I never drink either.

THEA. He doesn't.

HEDDA. But if I wanted you to?

LOEVBORG. It wouldn't make any difference.

HEDDA (*laughing*). So I have no power over you?

LOEVBORG. Not in that respect.

HEDDA. Well, you should have a drink for your own sake.

THEA. Hedda –

LOEVBORG. My sake?

HEDDA. Well, other people's . . .

THEA. Other people . . . ?

HEDDA. Who might think, deep down . . . that you don't have a mind of your own.

THEA. Oh Hedda . . .

LOEVBORG. People can believe whatever they want.

THEA. Whatever they want!

HEDDA. I could see it in the Judge just now.

LOEVBORG. What?

HEDDA. How scornful he looked when he saw you were afraid to have a drink.

LOEVBORG. I preferred to stay here and talk to you.

THEA. That seems reasonable, Hedda.

HEDDA. Oh, *reasonable*. The Judge didn't think that. I saw him wink at Tesman when you didn't dare go to their stupid dinner.

LOEVBORG. What do you mean, I didn't dare?

HEDDA. I'm saying it's what the Judge thought.

LOEVBORG. Well, let him think that.

HEDDA. So you're not going to go.

LOEVBORG. I'm staying here with the two of you.

THEA. Of course he is, Hedda.

HEDDA (*smiling*). So you're a man of iron discipline. High principles. That's what a man should be.

HEDDA *pats* THEA's *hand.*

It's what I told you this morning when you arrived in such a state.

LOEVBORG. What?

THEA. Hedda –

HEDDA. You can see for yourself now. There's no need for you to be terrified for him, I'm sure he can –

She stops.

So. So we can all have a jolly time.

LOEVBORG. What is all this?

THEA. Oh God, how could you, Hedda?

HEDDA. Sshhh! That frightful Judge can hear us.

LOEVBORG (to THEA). Terrified? For me?

THEA (*near to tears*). Oh Hedda . . .

LOEVBORG *looks hard at* THEA, *angry and contemptuous.*

LOEVBORG. So much for trusting me.

THEA. Oh Eilert, please –

EILERT *takes one of the glasses and drinks it down, followed by the other.*

LOEVBORG. Here's to you, Thea!

THEA (*quietly*). Oh Hedda . . . you wanted this to happen . . .

HEDDA. Are you insane?

LOEVBORG. And to you, Mrs Tesman! Thank you for being so honest. Here's to truth!

He drains the glass and goes to fill it. HEDDA *stops him.*

HEDDA. Don't. Not now. Remember you have a dinner party to go to.

THEA. No, no, no!

HEDDA. Ssshh! They can see you.

LOEVBORG *puts his glass down.*

LOEVBORG (*to* THEA). Tell me the truth –

THEA. Eilert . . .

LOEVBORG. Does your husband know you've followed me?

THEA. Oh Hedda . . .

LOEVBORG. Did you and the High Sheriff decide that you should come and spy on me? Was it his idea? Did he miss me in the office? Or did he need another hand at cards?

THEA (*sobbing*). Eilert, don't . . .

He fills his glass.

LOEVBORG. Here's to the health of the High Sheriff.

HEDDA. Don't, Eilert. Remember you're going out and you're going to read your book to Tesman.

He nods and puts his glass down calmly.

LOEVBORG. Stupid of me. Thea, I apologise, don't be angry, my sweet . . . collaborator. Don't worry, it'll be fine, you'll see, I'll be fine, I've been saved. By you, Thea.

THEA. Oh Eilert, thank God.

BRACK *is looking at his watch as he and* TESMAN *come in from the back room to pick up his hat and coat.*

BRACK. Well, Mrs Tesman, the time has come.

HEDDA. The time has come.

LOEVBORG (*rising*). For me too.

THEA. Don't, Eilert . . .

HEDDA (*pinching her arm*). They can hear you.

THEA. Ow!

LOEVBORG. Thank you for your generous invitation.

BRACK. You're coming?

LOEVBORG. Please.

BRACK. I'd be delighted.

LOEVBORG *picks up his manuscript and puts it in his overcoat pocket.*

LOEVBORG (*to* TESMAN). I want to show you one or two things before I give it to the printer.

TESMAN. Amazing! This'll be very enjoyable. Hedda, there won't be anyone to see Mrs Elvsted home, no?

HEDDA. I'm sure we'll manage.

LOEVBORG. Well, naturally, I'll come and take Mrs Elvsted home.

He comes closer to HEDDA.

Around ten o'clock, Mrs Tesman. Will that suit you?

HEDDA. Of course, that'll suit me fine.

TESMAN. Good. So everything's fine. But I won't be home by ten, Hedda.

HEDDA. You must stay as long as you like.

THEA. I'll wait here, Mr Loevborg.

LOEVBORG. Please do, Mrs Elvsted.

BRACK. Off to the carnival! I hope we have a 'merry' time, as a certain lovely lady puts it.

HEDDA. If only the lovely lady could be there, unseen . . .

BRACK. Why unseen?

HEDDA. To hear your unexpurgated merriment.

BRACK (*laughing*). I don't think I'd recommend that to a lovely lady.

TESMAN (*laughing*). Lovely lady, Hedda! Amazing!

BRACK. Ladies, goodbye.

LOEVBORG (*bowing*). Till ten o'clock.

BRACK, TESMAN *and* LOEVBORG *go out through the hall. It's now almost dark, just a faint grey light through the French windows.* BERTHE *comes in with a lit lamp which she puts on the table and then goes to the back room to clear the glasses.* THEA *paces nervously.*

THEA. What will happen, Hedda?

HEDDA. He'll come back at ten o'clock like Bacchus with vineleaves in his hair, wild and heady and confident.

THEA. I hope he'll be confident.

HEDDA. He'll be his own man. He'll have found his freedom again.

THEA. God willing.

HEDDA. He'll be his own man.

HEDDA *moves towards* THEA.

You can doubt him all you like, I have faith in him and I'll prove it.

THEA. What do you want from this, Hedda?

HEDDA. For once in my life I want to control a man's fate.

THEA. You already do.

HEDDA. I don't.

THEA. Not your husband's?

HEDDA. If only. You don't know how poor I am, while you are allowed to be so *rich* . . .

She throw her arms round THEA *with a furious passion.*

I think I will set fire to your hair, after all.

THEA. You frighten me, Hedda. Let go!

BERTHE *stands in the opening to the back room, staring impassively at them.*

BERTHE. I've laid for supper in the dining room, ma'am.

HEDDA. We're coming.

THEA. I want to go home! Let me go home now!

HEDDA. Oh shut up, you idiot! You'll have something to eat first and at ten o'clock, Eilert will be here. With vineleaves in his hair.

She drags THEA *towards the back room.*

Fade to black.

ACT THREE

It's dawn the next day. The shutters are closed. A thin dawn light is creeping into the room. The lamp on the table is still burning, its wick turned down low.

HEDDA *is lying asleep on the sofa, fully dressed, with a rug over her.* THEA *is sunk in the armchair by the stove, with her feet on a stool, wrapped in a large shawl.*

THEA *stirs, sits up and listens tensely. Then she sinks back and moans softly.*

THEA. Oh God, no . . .

BERTHE *tiptoes in from the hall door with a letter in her hand. They whisper.*

Has someone been here?

BERTHE. A girl come with this letter.

THEA (*reaching for the letter*). Give it to me!

BERTHE. It's for the Doctor, ma'am.

THEA. Oh . . .

BERTHE. His auntie's maid come with it. I'll leave it here.

BERTHE *puts the letter on the table.* THEA *nods.*

The lamp's smoking, better put 'er out.

THEA. Yes. It'll be light soon.

BERTHE. 'Tis light already.

She turns off the lamp.

THEA. Broad daylight and not back yet.

BERTHE. I could of told you.

THEA. What?

BERTHE. We've all heard tell of that lad, mind. He come back 'ere, he go off with them . . .

THEA. Ssshhh! You'll wake Mrs Tesman.

BERTHE. Let her sleep, poor soul. You want some wood on the fire?

THEA. Not for me. Thank you.

BERTHE. Right then.

She goes out quickly by the hall door, shutting it after her. HEDDA is woken by the noise. She sits up.

HEDDA. What is it?

THEA. The maid.

HEDDA (*looking round*). Here . . . Oh . . . yes.

She sits up.

What's the time, Thea?

THEA. Past seven.

HEDDA. What time did Tesman come in?

THEA. He didn't.

HEDDA. Didn't?

THEA. No one did.

THEA stands, anguished.

HEDDA. And we sat up for them till four and –

THEA. I waited . . . so . . . long . . .

HEDDA (*yawning*). We could have spared ourselves the trouble.

THEA. Did you sleep?

HEDDA. Quite well. Didn't you?

THEA. I couldn't, Hedda, I just couldn't . . .

HEDDA goes to THEA.

HEDDA. Shush . . . you mustn't worry . . . I know what's happened.

THEA. What? Hedda? What?

HEDDA. Well . . . it went on for ever at the Judge's, of course –

THEA. Oh heavens, yes, it must have done but –

HEDDA. And then Tesman didn't dare come back ringing the doorbell and crashing about the house . . . (*She laughs.*) Not too keen to show his face after such a thrash . . .

THEA. But where could he have gone?

HEDDA. To his auntie, of course. He still has a room there.

THEA. He can't have gone to his aunt, a letter just came from her. There.

HEDDA *picks up the letter.*

HEDDA. Mmm . . . it is from 'Aunt Juju'. Then he must have stayed with the Judge. And there he'll be, listening to Eilert, reading from his book with vineleaves in his hair.

THEA. Oh Hedda, you can't believe that.

HEDDA. Thea . . . you're a fool.

THEA. Yes. Yes, I probably am.

HEDDA. And you look desperately tired.

THEA. I am.

HEDDA. Then you must do what I tell you. Go to my bedroom and lie down . . .

THEA. I couldn't get to sleep, Hedda . . .

HEDDA. You can. If you try.

THEA. Your husband'll soon be home and I have to know –

HEDDA. I'll tell you when he comes.

THEA. You promise.

HEDDA. I promise. Go and sleep.

THEA. Thank you. I'll try.

HEDDA *indicates to* THEA *to go to the bedroom through the back room. Then she opens the shutters and light floods into the room. She takes a small mirror from the desk, looks into it and straightens her hair, then goes to the hall door and rings the bell beside it.* BERTHE *comes in.*

BERTHE. Ma'am?

HEDDA. I'm freezing. Make up the fire, will you?

BERTHE. Bless me, I'll have it warm in no time.

She rakes the embers and puts wood in the stove. Then stops: the doorbell is ringing.

Front door, ma'am.

HEDDA. You go. I'll see to the stove.

BERTHE. It'll burn up in no time.

HEDDA *kneels on the stool and puts wood into the stove.* TESMAN *comes in, looking tired and long-faced. He tiptoes towards the back room.*

HEDDA (*without looking up*). Good morning.

TESMAN. Hedda! Lord, you're up early, no?

HEDDA. Yes, I am up early today.

TESMAN. I was so sure you'd still be fast asleep. Amazing!

HEDDA. Quiet. Mrs Elvsted's asleep in the bedroom.

TESMAN. She stayed here?

HEDDA. Well, nobody came to take her home.

TESMAN. No, nobody came.

HEDDA *shuts the stove door and stands.*

HEDDA. Did you have fun at the Judge's?

TESMAN. You were worried about me, no?

HEDDA. No, that would never have occurred to me. Did you have fun at the Judge's?

TESMAN. Yes I did for once. Mostly at the beginning when Eilert read . . . D'you know, we were an hour early – amazing – so the Judge had a hundred and one things to see to but that's when Eilert read his book to me.

HEDDA *sits at the table.*

HEDDA. Then tell me about it.

TESMAN. Hedda, it's incredible, it must be one of the best things ever written. Amazing!

HEDDA (*cool*). Really.

TESMAN. D'you know, I have to say, Hedda, when he finished I had a horrible thought –

HEDDA. Horrible?

TESMAN. I envied him. I was jealous of Eilert for being able to write something like that. Can you imagine?

HEDDA. Yes. I can.

TESMAN. And to know that with all his . . . genius, I suppose . . . that he can't cope.

HEDDA. With what? The second-rate?

TESMAN. With his lack of control.

HEDDA. Why? What happened?

TESMAN. Well, it was positively . . . Bacchanalian, Hedda.

HEDDA. Did he wear vineleaves in his hair?

TESMAN. Vineleaves? What d'you . . . ? (*He shakes his head.*) He went on and on about the woman who'd 'inspired his work'. That's what he said, 'Inspired'.

HEDDA. Did he say who she was?

TESMAN. He must have meant Mrs Elvsted, must be her.

HEDDA. Where did you leave him?

TESMAN. On the way back. We all left together and Brack came too – to get some fresh air – and we all held Eilert up – he was really staggering . . .

HEDDA. I'm sure.

TESMAN. But this is the most extraordinary, Hedda, I mean sad, the saddest bit, I mean – I feel embarrassed, I mean for his sake –

HEDDA. Oh, for godsake, what!

TESMAN. I was having . . . they were ahead . . . I was running to catch them up, only a little way behind, two minutes perhaps, amazing . . .

HEDDA. Yes?

TESMAN. When I was running after them, d'you know what I saw at the side of the road?

HEDDA. How could I know?

TESMAN. You mustn't tell anyone, Hedda. Promise. For Eilert's sake.

He takes a large envelope from his overcoat pocket.

HEDDA. That's Eilert's manuscript.

TESMAN. It's his entire . . . irreplaceable . . . priceless
manuscript. Gone. Lost. And he never noticed. It's . . .
amazing. Tragic.

HEDDA. Why didn't you give it back to him straight away?

TESMAN. In the state he was in?

HEDDA. Didn't you tell anyone else you'd found it?

TESMAN. I didn't think I should for Eilert's sake.

HEDDA. So nobody knows that you have it.

TESMAN. And nobody must find out.

HEDDA. What did you say to him?

TESMAN. I didn't manage to say anything to him because
when we got into the centre of town he'd gone off with a
couple of the others –

HEDDA. Taken him home?

TESMAN. I suppose so. And Brack had disappeared.

HEDDA. And where did you gad about to after that?

TESMAN. Well, we went . . . um . . . home with one of the
chaps, who was . . . huh . . . we had 'morning coffee', well,
'night coffee', no? Oh Hedda, I'm exhausted – when
Eilert's slept it off I'll take this to him.

HEDDA *reaches out for the manuscript.*

HEDDA. No, don't! I mean not yet. Let me read it first.

TESMAN. Hedda . . . Hedda, sweetheart, I couldn't do that.

HEDDA. You daren't.

TESMAN. Just imagine how he'll feel when he wakes up and
finds it's gone. It's his only copy!

She looks at him steadily.

HEDDA. It couldn't be re-written?

TESMAN. I shouldn't think so, the fire of inspiration, you
know . . .

HEDDA. Yes, I suppose so. Oh, by the way, there's a letter for
you.

TESMAN. Amazing.

HEDDA (*giving it to him*). It came earlier this morning.

TESMAN. It's from Aunt Juju.

He puts the manuscript down in the armchair and opens the letter.

Oh no! Oh Hedda, she says Aunt Rena's dying.

HEDDA. It's hardly a surprise.

TESMAN. She says I must hurry if I want to see her. I must run.

HEDDA (*suppressing a smile*). Run?

TESMAN. Oh Hedda, sweet Hedda, if only you'd come with me.

HEDDA (*wearily*). Don't. I loathe illness and death. It's all so ugly.

TESMAN. Oh. Well then . . . Now, where's my hat? Hall. Coat? Oh, got it on. Oh Hedda, I hope I'm not too late, no?

HEDDA. You'd better run.

BERTHE *comes to the hall door.*

BERTHE. His Honour Judge Brack's here.

TESMAN. I can't see him.

HEDDA. I can. Ask him to come in. (*In a fierce whisper.*) The manuscript!

She picks it up.

TESMAN. Give it to me.

HEDDA. I'll put it here.

HEDDA *puts the manuscript on a bookshelf above the desk, while* TESMAN *is struggling to get his gloves on.* BRACK *comes into the room.*

Well, you're an early bird.

BRACK. D'you think? (*To* TESMAN.) Are you going out?

TESMAN. My aunt, Aunt Rena, she's . . . um . . . very serious.

BRACK. Oh Lord, well, you mustn't let me hold you up –

TESMAN. I'm sorry, I must run. Goodbye, goodbye.

He runs out, slamming the front door behind him.

HEDDA. So a rather more than merry time at your house last night.

BRACK. You see – (*Opening his overcoat.*) I haven't changed.

HEDDA. You too.

BRACK. Yes indeed. What's Tesman told you about last night?

HEDDA. Oh, some tedious stuff about drinking coffee somewhere.

BRACK. Ah, yes, the coffee party. But without Eilert Loevborg perhaps?

HEDDA. They'd taken him home.

BRACK. Tesman had?

HEDDA. No, a couple of the others, he said.

BRACK (*smiling*). George Tesman. Good, decent, trusting.

HEDDA. Yes, God knows he's that all right. Has something happened?

BRACK. You could say.

HEDDA. Why don't you sit?

BRACK *sits at the table, near her.*

Well?

BRACK. I had a special reason for keeping an eye on my guests last night, well, some of them at least.

HEDDA. You mean Eilert?

BRACK. I do indeed.

HEDDA. Well . . . ?

BRACK. Do you have any idea where Eilert and some of the others spent the rest of the night?

HEDDA. Will it make me blush?

BRACK. Oh, I don't think so. They ended up at a very lively soirée.

HEDDA. Of the animated variety?

BRACK. Of the utmost animation.

HEDDA. And?

BRACK. Loevborg had been sent an invitation which I knew about. But he'd . . . declined. Because he's reformed, of course.

HEDDA. Saved by Mrs Elvsted. But he went.

BRACK. He went. You see, the spirit had started to move him at my house.

HEDDA. I heard he was inspired.

BRACK. Quite violently. And I suppose he changed his mind. We men aren't always as disciplined as we should be.

HEDDA. I'm sure you're an exception but Eilert –

BRACK. To cut to the chase – he ended up at Mademoiselle Diana's.

HEDDA. Mademoiselle Diana's?

BRACK. She was holding a, um, soirée. For a select group of girls and boys.

HEDDA. Does she have red hair?

BRACK. She does.

HEDDA. And she's a sort of . . . singer?

BRACK. Among other accomplishments. Diana is a huntress. Of men, Madame Hedda. I know you've heard of her. Eilert was one of her most fanatical enthusiasts.

HEDDA. And what happened?

BRACK. He became less so. And she switched from kisses to blows.

HEDDA. She hit Eilert?

BRACK. He accused her – or her friends – of stealing his wallet and other stuff and by all accounts made a ghastly scene.

HEDDA. How did it end?

BRACK. It ended with a fight. Ladies *and* gentlemen. Luckily the police intervened.

HEDDA. The police came?

BRACK. Looks like a costly caper for Master Loevborg. Idiot.

HEDDA. Oh . . .

BRACK. He seems to have hit a policeman and torn his
uniform. So he ended up at the police station.

HEDDA. How do you know all this?

BRACK. From the police.

HEDDA *stands, head raised, staring upwards.*

HEDDA. So there were no vineleaves in his hair.

BRACK. Vineleaves?

HEDDA. Why were you so keen to investigate Eilert's
movements?

BRACK. Well, for a start, it wouldn't be entirely comfortable
for it to emerge in court that he'd come straight from my
house.

HEDDA. Will he go to court?

BRACK. Perhaps – it's neither here nor there. As a friend of
the family, I thought I should tell you about Eilert's
adventures.

HEDDA. Why?

BRACK. Because I suspect he'll use you as a sort of . . .
camouflage.

HEDDA. What do you mean?

BRACK. Oh, for godsake, Hedda, open your eyes. Mrs Elvsted
is here and she won't be going back to her husband.

HEDDA. Well, if there *was* anything going on between those
two there are any number of places where they can meet.

BRACK. There isn't a respectable house in town that will let
them in.

HEDDA. And that includes mine?

BRACK. It does. I would be deeply displeased if that man
were welcomed here. If I found that he was intruding –

HEDDA. Intruding on the triangle?

BRACK. It would be like losing a home.

HEDDA *looks at him steadily and smiles.*

HEDDA. I see. You want to be the only cock in the yard.

BRACK *nods slowly and speaks very quietly.*

BRACK. That's right. And I shall fight for it in any way that I have to.

HEDDA (*not smiling*). You're a very dangerous man.

BRACK. Am I?

HEDDA. I'm only grateful you have no hold over me.

BRACK. Perhaps not. At the moment.

HEDDA. Are you threatening me?

He stands.

BRACK. Far from it. The triangle should be a matter of mutual consent.

HEDDA. Exactly.

BRACK. Well, I've said what I came here to say. I must be going. Goodbye, Mrs Tesman.

He goes to the French windows and opens them.

HEDDA. Are you going through the garden?

BRACK. It's shorter.

HEDDA. And devious.

BRACK. True. Being devious can be . . . exciting.

HEDDA. So can firing a pistol.

BRACK. Oh, I don't think people shoot tame roosters.

HEDDA. Especially if one only has one.

They nod to each other, laughing. He goes out and she shuts the doors after him. HEDDA stands for a moment, quite still, looking out. Then she goes to the back room and peers in. She goes to the desk, takes the manuscript from the bookcase and is just going to look through it when she hears BERTHE's voice, speaking loudly in the hall. She listens, then puts the manuscript in the door of the desk and locks it.

BERTHE. You can't go in, not in that state.

LOEVBORG. I'm going in! Get out, get out of my way!

LOEVBORG, *wearing his coat, flings open the door from the hall. He looks wild. He sees* HEDDA *at the desk and he controls himself and bows.*

HEDDA. You're a little late for Thea, Mr Loevborg.

LOEVBORG. Or a little early for you. Forgive me.

HEDDA. How do you know she's here?

LOEVBORG. They told me at her boarding house that she hadn't come back.

HEDDA *goes to the table.*

HEDDA. And how did they react when you asked?

LOEVBORG. How did they . . . ?

HEDDA. I mean, did they seem . . . disapproving?

LOEVBORG. Oh, you mean I'm dragging her into the gutter. No, they didn't. I suppose Tesman isn't up?

HEDDA. I don't think he is.

LOEVBORG. When did he get home?

HEDDA. Late.

LOEVBORG. Did he tell you anything?

HEDDA. What a merry time you had at the Judge's.

LOEVBORG. Nothing else?

HEDDA. I don't think so. I was half-asleep . . .

THEA *runs in from the back room, tousled, half-asleep.*

THEA. Eilert! At last!

LOEVBORG. Too late.

THEA. What? What?

LOEVBORG. Everything. I'm finished.

THEA. Don't say that.

LOEVBORG. You'd say it yourself if you knew what'd happened.

THEA. I don't want to know.

HEDDA (*to* LOEVBORG). I'll go.

LOEVBORG. Stay.

THEA. I don't want to know!

LOEVBORG. It's not about last night!

A silence.

THEA. What . . . ?

LOEVBORG. We must stop seeing each other.

THEA. Stop seeing . . . ?

LOEVBORG. I don't need you any more.

THEA. How can you say that you don't need me? We have to go on working together.

LOEVBORG. I'm not going to work any more.

THEA. What'll I do with my life?

LOEVBORG. You've got to live as if you'd never heard of me.

THEA. I can't!

LOEVBORG. You have to. You have to go home –

THEA. I won't. I have to be with you. Wherever you are. I won't let you push me away. I have to be with you when the book comes out.

HEDDA. Ah yes, the book . . .

LOEVBORG. The book. The book I wrote with Thea. Our book.

THEA. It is, it is ours and I want to be with you and share your joy when they applaud you and honour –

LOEVBORG. Thea, the book won't come out.

HEDDA. Ah . . .

THEA. What do you mean?

LOEVBORG. The book won't come out.

THEA. Eilert, where's our text?

HEDDA. Yes, the text . . .

THEA. Where's the manuscript?

LOEVBORG. Thea, please, please don't ask me that.

THEA. I want to know, I have to know, now!

LOEVBORG. The manuscript . . . Right. Our manuscript . . . has been . . . I've torn it into a thousand pieces.

THEA. Oh no, noooooooooo!

HEDDA (*involuntarily*). But that's not –

LOEVBORG. Not true?

LOEVBORG *looks steadily at* HEDDA.

Is that what you think?

HEDDA. Well, if you say it is. It just seems so . . . incredible.

LOEVBORG. But it's true.

THEA. Hedda, oh God, Hedda, oh God . . . he's destroyed his work . . .

LOEVBORG. I've destroyed my life, why not my work?

THEA. So that's what you did last night?

LOEVBORG. I tore the pages into a thousand pieces and I flung them in the fiord. Into the clear saltwater. And they can drift there, in the currents and the tides, until they dissolve. Into nothing. The way I will.

THEA. All my life, Eilert, this is going to feel like you've killed a baby.

LOEVBORG. You're right. I've murdered a child.

THEA. But it was my child as well.

HEDDA (*under her breath*). Oh . . . the child . . .

THEA *sighs deeply and nods as if convincing herself of something.*

THEA. Well, it's over. I'll go now, Hedda.

HEDDA. Home?

THEA. I don't know. The future's just a . . .

She looks around for her coat and hat, remembers they're in the hall and moves towards the door.

. . . blank.

THEA *goes out. The front door closes and there's a silence.*

HEDDA. You're not going to take her back to her boarding house, Mr Loevborg?

LOEVBORG. You want her to be seen with me in public?

HEDDA. Look, I don't know what went on last night, but is it completely irrevocable?

LOEVBORG. Oh, last night won't be the last. I'll go back to the . . . drinking and the . . . women and . . . But the curse of it, the worst thing, is that I don't have the appetite for it. To raise a fist to the world. She's sapped my will for it. I can't spit in the world's face any more.

HEDDA (*looking straight ahead*). An innocent little fool and she's managed to change a man's life.

She looks at him.

Even so, I don't know how you can be so cruel to her.

LOEVBORG. Don't say that.

HEDDA. To destroy what made her life worth living? You don't call that cruel?

LOEVBORG. Hedda, listen.

HEDDA. I'm listening.

LOEVBORG. Promise me you'll never tell Thea what I'm going to tell you.

HEDDA. I promise.

LOEVBORG. Right. Well. What I've just said wasn't true.

HEDDA. About your manuscript?

LOEVBORG. I haven't torn it up. Or thrown it in the fiord.

HEDDA. No? Where is it then?

LOEVBORG. It's destroyed. Gone. Completely.

HEDDA. I don't understand.

LOEVBORG. Thea said I'd murdered a child.

HEDDA. Yes.

LOEVBORG. But killing your child's not the worst thing a father can do, is it?

HEDDA. Isn't it?

LOEVBORG. I didn't want Thea to hear.

HEDDA. What?

LOEVBORG. Just imagine, imagine that after a night of drinking and whoring, in the early hours a man comes back home and says to his . . . to the mother of his child: I've seen such and such, done such and such, been here been there, and I took our child with me into those places and now, now I can't find the child, I've lost our child, I don't know who has our child, I don't know what they've done to our child . . .

HEDDA. Eilert, it's a book. A book.

LOEVBORG. Thea's life was in it . . .

HEDDA. Yes, I understand that . . .

LOEVBORG. . . . her whole heart and soul. So you can understand that I can't ever look her in the face again.

HEDDA. So what will you do?

LOEVBORG. Nothing. End it all. As soon as I can.

HEDDA *moves towards* LOEVBORG.

HEDDA. Eilert, listen . . . if you . . . when you do it, will you do it beautifully?

LOEVBORG. Beautifully?

He smiles.

With vineleaves in my hair?

HEDDA. Oh, I don't believe in that nonsense any more. Make it beautiful. One beautiful gesture. You must go now. Goodbye, Eilert, you mustn't come here again.

LOEVBORG. Then . . . adieu, Mrs Tesman. Please give your husband my regards.

As he turns to leave, HEDDA *runs to the desk and opens the drawer where the manuscript is.*

HEDDA. Wait. I want to give you something.

She unlocks the drawer.

It's something to remember me by.

She takes one of her pistols from the drawer and goes to
LOEVBORG.

LOEVBORG. This? Is this my souvenir?

She nods slowly.

HEDDA. Don't you recognise it? I aimed it at you once.

LOEVBORG. You should have used it.

HEDDA. You use it.

He puts the pistol in his pocket.

Make it beautiful. Promise me, Eilert. (*Softly.*) Eilert
Loevborg.

LOEVBORG. Goodbye, Hedda Gabler.

He leaves. The front door closes. HEDDA *listens for a
moment and then goes to the desk where she takes out the
manuscript, pulls out some pages and looks at them. Then
she walks across the room to the stove.*

*She pulls the armchair up to the stove and sits with the
manuscript in her lap. After a moment she opens the door of
the stove, takes some pages and whispers as she throws
them into the fire:*

HEDDA. I'm burning your baby, Thea. Thea with the golden
curls.

She throws more pages on the flames.

I'm burning the child that you had with him.

She throws the rest of the pages in.

I'm burning your child. I'm burning the baby.

Fade to black.

ACT FOUR

It's evening. The drawing room is in darkness; the back room is lit by a lamp hanging over the table. The shutters at the French windows are closed.

HEDDA, *dressed in black, paces to and fro in the dark drawing room. Then she goes into the back room, plays some chords on the piano, then comes back into the drawing room. BERTHE comes in with a lighted lamp that she sets down on the table in the drawing room. She's been crying and she has black ribbons in her cap. She goes out to the hall.*

HEDDA *goes to the French windows, opens the shutters and looks out into the darkness.* MISS TESMAN, *dressed in mourning – hat and veil – comes in from the hall.* HEDDA *goes to her, her hand outstretched.*

MISS TESMAN. Well, Hedda, here I am. My poor sister's struggle is over and I'm wearing the badge of grief.

HEDDA (*of her black dress*). Well, as you see, I've already heard. George sent me a message.

MISS TESMAN. He promised me he would but I thought: no, I must go to Hedda, I must take the message of death to the house of life.

HEDDA. That was very kind of you.

MISS TESMAN. I wish that Rena hadn't passed away just at this moment when Hedda's home should be a place of joy.

HEDDA. Did she have a peaceful death?

MISS TESMAN. A beautiful one. The end came so calmly and she was blessed by being able to say goodbye to George. Is he back yet?

HEDDA. No, he said in his note that I shouldn't expect him too soon. Do sit down.

MISS TESMAN. Thank you, dear Hedda, but I mustn't stay. I have to dress her and lay her out. She must look beautiful for her burial.

HEDDA. Is there nothing I can do to help?

MISS TESMAN. Don't even think of it. You mustn't let your hands touch death and your mind mustn't be bothered with such thoughts. You must –

HEDDA. Well, you can't control your thoughts –

MISS TESMAN. You must accept that's how the world goes. While I'm sewing a shroud for Rena, there will be sewing for another purpose here, thank the good Lord.

GEORGE TESMAN *comes in from the hall.*

HEDDA. Not a minute too soon.

TESMAN. Aunt Juju! You're here with Hedda. Amazing!

MISS TESMAN. Dearest Georgie, I was just about to go. Did you manage to do everything I asked you to?

TESMAN. I'm sorry, I've forgotten half of it. I'll have to run in tomorrow, I'm so confused today, my head's all over the place.

MISS TESMAN. Dear dear boy, you mustn't react like this.

TESMAN. How should I react?

MISS TESMAN. You must find joy in the sadness.

TESMAN. You mean Aunt Rena?

HEDDA. You'll be lonely now, Miss Tesman.

MISS TESMAN. For now, yes. But poor Rena's little room won't be empty for long.

TESMAN. Who will you put in it?

MISS TESMAN. Oh, there's always someone who needs caring for, I'm afraid.

HEDDA. You'll bear that cross again?

MISS TESMAN. Dear me, God forgive you, it's not a cross.

HEDDA. Looking after a total stranger . . . ?

MISS TESMAN. You soon make friends with people when they're ill. I need someone to live for. And, thanks be to God, there'll be a thing or two here for an old aunt to lend a hand with.

HEDDA. Please don't start interfering –

TESMAN. The three of us could be so happy if . . .

HEDDA. If what?

TESMAN. It'll sort itself out, I'm sure. I hope. No?

There's a short, embarrassed silence.

MISS TESMAN. Well. You've things to discuss, I can see. (*Smiling.*) Perhaps Hedda has something to tell you, George.

She starts for the door.

I must get back for Rena.

She stops, shaking her head.

It's so strange . . . Rena's still in the house and she's with my dear dead brother.

TESMAN. Amazing, Aunt Juju, no?

TESMAN *sees her out the front door and then returns from the hall.* HEDDA *stares hard at* TESMAN.

HEDDA. I think you're more upset about her death than she is.

TESMAN. It's not just that, it's Eilert.

HEDDA. What's happened?

TESMAN. I went round this afternoon to tell him that I had his manuscript.

HEDDA. You didn't see him?

TESMAN. He wasn't there. But then I ran into Mrs Elvsted. She told me he'd been here this morning.

HEDDA. Just after you went.

TESMAN. Apparently he said he'd torn up his manuscript, no?

HEDDA. That's what he said.

TESMAN. But you must have told him we had it?

HEDDA. No. Did you tell Mrs Elvsted that we did?

He shakes his head.

TESMAN. You should have told him, Hedda. He'll be in such a desperate state he might – oh God, give me the manuscript, I'll run over to him. Where is it?

HEDDA *leans against the armchair, impassive.*

HEDDA. It's gone.

TESMAN. What d'you mean, 'gone'?

HEDDA. I burnt it.

TESMAN *leaps up.*

TESMAN. You burnt it? You burnt Eilert's book!

HEDDA. Don't shout, the maid'll hear you.

TESMAN. Burnt? Oh dear God, no. No no no no no, I don't believe it . . .

HEDDA. Well, it's true.

TESMAN. Have you got any idea what you've done, Hedda? It's a crime, don't you realise that? Ask the Judge, ask him!

HEDDA. I wouldn't advise you to mention it to him. Or anyone.

TESMAN. How could you do something so . . . insane? How could you do something like that? Why?

HEDDA *conceals an almost imperceptible smile.*

HEDDA. I did it for you . . . George.

TESMAN. For me?

HEDDA. You came back and told me he'd read his book to you . . .

TESMAN. Yes?

HEDDA. . . . and you told me you were jealous of him.

TESMAN. Oh God, I didn't mean literally.

HEDDA. It doesn't matter. I didn't want anyone to overshadow you.

TESMAN. Is that true? Really true? I've never seen . . . I mean, I never realised you loved me like –

HEDDA. Well, you'd better realise NOW!

She breaks off violently.

Oh, talk to your aunt, I'm sure she can spell it out for you.

TESMAN. Do I understand you properly?

He claps his hands.

Oh God! It's not possible! No!

HEDDA. Don't shout, the maid can hear you.

TESMAN *reels about, laughing in joy, while* HEDDA *writhes in desperation.*

TESMAN. The maid? That's hilarious, Hedda. 'The maid.' *Berthe*! I'll tell her myself!

HEDDA (*shouting*). I can't bear it! I can't bear living with this!

TESMAN. With what, Hedda? What?

HEDDA (*controlled again*). With all this . . . absurdity, George.

TESMAN. Is it absurd that I'm so happy? Well, perhaps it's best that I don't tell Berthe yet.

HEDDA. Oh, tell Berthe, why not?

TESMAN. No, you're right, that would be wrong. Aunt Juju must be told first –

He stops.

You called me George. Amazing. Aunt Juju will be so . . . happy. So happy.

HEDDA. When she hears I've burnt Eilert Loevborg's book for you?

TESMAN. No, of course, you're right, she mustn't know, no one must know about the manuscript. I can't get over it, you did it for *me*! I wish Aunt Juju knew. You did it for *me*! D'you think . . . (*He laughs.*) . . . do you think all young wives in your state are like this? No?

HEDDA. Why don't you ask Aunt Juju?

TESMAN. Yes, yes, I will . . .

TESMAN *is out of breath for a moment and is caught by a wave of unease.*

Oh God . . . Eilert's book. Oh God, I can't bear to think of him . . .

THEA *runs in from the hall, breathlessly.*

THEA. Hedda, I'm so sorry to come back –

HEDDA. What's happened, Thea?

TESMAN. Is it Eilert?

THEA. I'm terrified something awful's happened.

HEDDA *grabs* THEA*'s arm.*

HEDDA / TESMAN. What? What's happened? / What makes you think so?

THEA. When I got back to my boarding house they were talking about him – there are terrible rumours about him everywhere.

TESMAN. I heard. They can't be true, I was with him. He went home.

HEDDA. What did they say at the boarding house?

THEA. They stopped talking when they saw me. I didn't dare ask.

TESMAN *paces uneasily.*

TESMAN. I'm sure . . . I'm sure you heard wrong, Mrs Elvsted, I'm sure it wasn't –

THEA. It was him. I know. I heard something about a hospital –

TESMAN. Hospital!

HEDDA. You can't have.

THEA. I was so frightened I went to his lodgings and I asked for him.

HEDDA. How could you do that, Thea . . .

THEA. What else could I do? I had to know.

TESMAN. But you didn't see him, no?

THEA. They didn't know what had happened to him. He hadn't been seen since yesterday evening.

TESMAN. Yesterday?

THEA. Something must've happened.

TESMAN. Hedda, I wonder if I should go into town, perhaps make some enquiries . . .

HEDDA. No. Stay out of it.

The hall door is opened by BERTHE. JUDGE BRACK *comes in. He looks solemn.*

TESMAN. Oh Judge . . . it's you.

BRACK. I had to see you.

TESMAN. You've obviously heard about Aunt Rena.

BRACK. Yes, yes, that too.

TESMAN. It's tragic, no?

BRACK. It rather depends on your perspective.

TESMAN. Has something else happened?

BRACK. Yes.

HEDDA. Another tragedy?

BRACK. That depends on your perspective too, Mrs Tesman.

THEA. It's something about Eilert.

BRACK *looks at her steadily.*

BRACK. Have you heard something . . . ?

THEA (*confused*). No, I . . . no . . .

TESMAN. For God sake, tell us!

BRACK *shrugs wearily.*

BRACK. I'm sorry . . . Eilert's been taken to hospital. He doesn't have long.

THEA / TESMAN. Oh God! Oh God! / What?

HEDDA (*involuntarily*). So soon?

THEA. We parted in anger, Hedda!

HEDDA (*whispers*). Sssshhhh, Thea . . .

THEA *is oblivious to* HEDDA.

THEA. I must go to him, I have to go to him before he dies.

BRACK. They won't let anyone see him . . .

THEA. Tell me what happened.

TESMAN. He can't have . . . It can't be . . . suicide, can it?

HEDDA. I'm sure it is.

TESMAN. How can you be . . . ?

BRACK *looks at* HEDDA *directly.*

BRACK. I'm afraid you've guessed correctly, Mrs Tesman.

THEA. Oh no . . .

TESMAN. Suicide . . . amazing.

HEDDA. Shot himself.

BRACK. Correct, Mrs Tesman.

THEA *tries to pull herself together.*

THEA. When was it?

BRACK. This afternoon. Between three and four.

TESMAN. But good heavens – where?

For a moment BRACK *looks confused.*

BRACK. Where? . . . Well, at his lodgings.

THEA. He couldn't have. I was there later.

BRACK. Well, somewhere else then, I don't know. I only know that he was found . . . He'd um . . . shot himself. Through the heart.

THEA. What a terrible way to die.

HEDDA. Through the heart?

BRACK. That's what I said.

HEDDA. Not the head?

BRACK. The heart, Mrs Tesman.

HEDDA. Well, yes, the heart is good too.

BRACK. What?

HEDDA *shakes her head dismissively.*

TESMAN. It's a bad wound, no?

BRACK. He's probably . . . gone already.

THEA. I'm sure of it. I know, I know it's over . . . Oh Hedda, I know . . .

TESMAN (*to* BRACK). How do you know all this?

BRACK (*curtly*). I had some business with the police.

HEDDA. Thank God!

TESMAN. Hedda, what –

HEDDA. It's beautiful.

BRACK. Mrs Tesman . . .

TESMAN. Beautiful?

THEA. How can you call it beautiful?

HEDDA. He paid his debts. He dared to do . . . what he had to do.

THEA. He did it because he was mad.

TESMAN. He was desperate.

HEDDA. No, he wasn't, I know he wasn't.

THEA. He was! That's why he tore up his manuscript.

BRACK *starts suddenly.*

BRACK. He tore up his manuscript?

THEA. Last night.

TESMAN *leans close to* HEDDA *and whispers something to her; she shakes her head defiantly.*

BRACK. How bizarre.

There's a silence. BRACK *looks at* HEDDA. TESMAN *starts to wander round the room in agony.*

TESMAN. How could he have . . . died like that without leaving the thing that would have made his name?

THEA. I wish . . . there was a way of putting it together again.

TESMAN. Oh God, yes, I'd give anything in the world for that.

THEA. It could be done.

TESMAN. How?

THEA *searches her handbag and extracts some pages.*

THEA. I kept his notes.

HEDDA. Oh!

TESMAN. You kept them, no?

THEA. I took them with me when I left, they've been in my bag since then.

TESMAN. Let me see.

She hands him the scrumpled bunch of notes.

THEA. They're a mess.

TESMAN. I wonder if we could sort them out together . . .

THEA. We have to try.

TESMAN. We can do it. We will! I'll devote my life to it.

HEDDA. Your life, George?

TESMAN. Well, all the spare time I have. My own work'll have to wait, Hedda. You understand, no? I owe it to Eilert.

HEDDA. Perhaps you do.

TESMAN. We must pull ourselves together. We mustn't brood over what's happened, no?

THEA. Yes . . .

TESMAN. We must be calm and clear-headed.

THEA. . . . Yes, I'll try.

TESMAN. Let's have a look at the notes, shall we? Shall we . . . ?

He goes towards the table to sit.

No, let's go in the back room. Do excuse us, Judge.

THEA. If only we can do it . . .

She follows TESMAN *into the back room where she takes her hat and coat off and they sit at the small table, their backs to the others, under the hanging lamp. They start to sort the papers with an eager enthusiasm.*

HEDDA goes up to the stove, taps it lightly with her toe and sits in the armchair. BRACK watches her and then moves towards her.

HEDDA (*barely audible*). What a deliverance . . .

BRACK. I suppose for him it is.

HEDDA. For me. To know that someone can do something brave, something that's entirely of their own volition. Free will's a beautiful thing.

BRACK (*smiles*). Mmm . . . Madame Hedda –

HEDDA. I know what you're going to say but at heart you're as middle-class as . . . oh, never mind.

BRACK. Eilert Loevborg meant more to you than you like to admit. Even to yourself? Am I right?

HEDDA. I don't answer questions like that, I only know that Eilert Loevborg was brave enough to live life on his own terms. This is his triumph, this beautiful act. He had the strength to get up from the table, to break with life, do it so young . . .

BRACK. It pains me, Madame Hedda, to have to wean you off your fairytale.

HEDDA. Fairytale?

BRACK. It wouldn't have survived the truth anyway.

HEDDA. And what's that?

BRACK. He didn't shoot himself intentionally.

HEDDA. He didn't?

BRACK. No, it didn't happen quite as I told it.

HEDDA. You've been hiding something. What?

BRACK. For Mrs Elvsted's sake I made one or two . . . improvements to the tale.

HEDDA. What?

BRACK. First. He's already dead.

HEDDA. In hospital?

BRACK. Without regaining consciousness.

HEDDA. What else?

BRACK. He didn't shoot himself in his room.

HEDDA. That's neither here nor there.

BRACK. I wouldn't agree. He was shot in Mademoiselle Diana's bedroom.

HEDDA *jumps up, then sinks back again.*

HEDDA. That's just not possible! He can't have been there again today.

BRACK. He was there this afternoon. He came to fetch something that he claimed she'd taken from him. He gibbered about some lost child –

HEDDA. Oh . . . that . . .

BRACK. I wondered if he'd meant his manuscript but apparently he'd already destroyed that himself, so it must have been his wallet.

HEDDA. It must. And he was found there . . . there?

BRACK. Yes, there. With a pistol in his jacket pocket that had fired the shot that killed him.

HEDDA. Yes. In the heart.

BRACK. No. Not in the heart. Here.

BRACK *points to his groin.* HEDDA *looks up at* BRACK *with disgust.*

HEDDA. How common. Everything I touch seems to become stupid and vulgar.

BRACK. There's something else too, just as vulgar.

HEDDA. What?

BRACK. The pistol . . .

HEDDA. What!

BRACK. . . . must have been stolen.

HEDDA *jumps up.*

HEDDA. That's a lie! He didn't steal it!

BRACK. He *has* to have stolen it, it's the only possible explanation. Ssshhh!

As HEDDA *is about to reply,* TESMAN *and* THEA *get up from the table in the back room.* TESMAN *has sheaves of papers in both hands.*

TESMAN. Hedda, it's hard to see under that lamp and we need some more space. Amazing.

HEDDA. Yes. Amazing.

TESMAN. Could we possibly use your desk, no?

HEDDA. Of course. Oh wait! Let me tidy it first.

TESMAN. You don't need to do that, Hedda, there's plenty of room. We'll use the table too.

HEDDA. I said I'd tidy it. This can all go on the piano.

He starts to spread papers on the round table as HEDDA *goes to the desk and pulls something from a drawer, covers it with sheets of music from the bookshelf and takes it all into the back room, where she puts it down on the piano.*

There!

TESMAN *moves the lamp to the desk, as* THEA *takes a chair from the table to the desk, and picks up some pages from the table. The two of them sit close together poring over the notes, occasionally pointing something out to each other; now and again, one or other of them gets up to take another page from the table.*

HEDDA *comes back in. She stands behind* THEA, *gently stroking her golden curls.*

How's the memorial going?

THEA (*looking up at* HEDDA). It's just so hard.

TESMAN. But we have to do it. And it's what I do: I organise other people's work.

HEDDA *goes over to the stove and sits, bent over, on the footstool.* BRACK *stands above her, leaning on the armchair. She whispers.*

HEDDA. What did you mean about the pistol?

BRACK. That he must have stolen it?

HEDDA. Yes.

BRACK. There's no other possible explanation.

HEDDA. Of what?

BRACK. He was here this morning, wasn't he?

HEDDA. Yes.

BRACK. Were you alone with him?

HEDDA. For a while.

BRACK. Did you go out of the room when he was here?

HEDDA. No.

BRACK. Think about it: did you leave him – for a moment – alone in the room?

HEDDA. I was in the hall, maybe, for a moment.

BRACK. And where were the pistols?

HEDDA. They were locked in –

She stops, looks at him.

BRACK. Well, Madame Hedda?

HEDDA. The case was lying there on the desk.

BRACK. And have you looked to see if both pistols are in there?

HEDDA. No.

BRACK. You needn't bother, I saw the pistol on the corpse. And I recognised it from yesterday. And other occasions.

HEDDA. Have you got it?

BRACK. The police have it.

HEDDA. What will they do with it?

BRACK. Trace the owner.

HEDDA. Will they succeed?

He sits on the arm of the chair and leans over her.

BRACK. Not if I keep quiet, Hedda Gabler.

She looks up but avoids his eyes.

HEDDA. And if you don't?

BRACK. You could always tell them it's stolen.

HEDDA. I would rather die.

BRACK (*smiling*). People say things like that, they never do them.

HEDDA. When they trace the owner, what happens then?

BRACK. Then there's the scandal . . .

HEDDA. Scandal?

BRACK. . . . that you have such a horror of. You'd have to appear in court alongside Mademoiselle Diana, who would have to explain the saga. Was it an accident or was it manslaughter? Did the pistol go off when he was trying to get it out of his pocket? Or did she grab the pistol, shoot him, then put it back in his pocket? That would be in character, she's a big girl, Diana.

HEDDA. I'm not interested in the vulgar details.

BRACK. But you won't be able to avoid the question: why did you give him the pistol? And what conclusions do you think they'll draw?

HEDDA *lowers her head.*

HEDDA. I hadn't thought of that.

BRACK. Well, luckily there's no danger as long as I keep quiet.

She looks up at him.

HEDDA. I'm in your power then. For ever.

BRACK. Hedda, darling, I shan't take advantage of you.

HEDDA. But I won't be free. You'll own me. I'll be your slave.

She jumps up.

I won't, I won't let you.

BRACK. Oh, people usually find a way of putting up with what they can't change . . .

HEDDA. People do, do they?

HEDDA *goes towards the desk. She mimics* TESMAN, *suppressing a smile as she does so.*

Well, George, the work's going well, no?

TESMAN. Too early to say, there's months of work here.

HEDDA. Amazing.

She strokes THEA's *golden curls.*

Don't you find it odd, Thea, that you're working alongside Tesman the way you did with Eilert Loevborg?

THEA. If I could only inspire your husband too . . .

HEDDA. Oh, I'm sure you will. In time.

TESMAN. I feel a bit, well . . . you know, inspired already, Hedda. Why don't you go and chat to the Judge?

HEDDA. So I'm no use to you two at all?

TESMAN. No. (*Calling to him.*) You'll have to keep Hedda company, Judge.

BRACK. It will be pure pleasure.

HEDDA. Thank you, but I'm a bit tired. I'll lie down in there for a little while.

HEDDA *looks at* BRACK *for a moment and then goes into the back room. There's a silence, then the sound of a wild dance on the piano: 'Danse Macabre' by Saint-Saëns.* THEA *jumps up in irritation.*

THEA. Ooooh, what's that!

TESMAN *runs to the back room.*

TESMAN. Hedda, not tonight. Think about Aunt Rena. And Eilert too.

He goes back to the desk and then HEDDA *comes back into the room, a hand on the doorway.*

HEDDA. And what about Aunt Juju? And all the rest of them. From this moment on I'll be silent. Not one word.

HEDDA *pauses a moment, looks at them all and then slowly leaves the room.* TESMAN *settles at the desk.*

TESMAN. I think she's upset seeing us doing this gloomy work, don't you? I'll tell you what, you could move into Aunt Juju's and I could come round every evening and we could work there, no?

THEA. That might be best.

HEDDA (*from the back room*). I can hear you. Every word. What will I do here every evening?

TESMAN (*passing papers to* THEA). I'm sure the Judge will come to visit you.

BRACK. Oh, it'll be a pleasure. Every evening, we'll have a merry time . . .

HEDDA (*from the back room*). Yes, that's what you want, isn't it? To be the cock of the walk –

There's a shot. It's violently loud in the drawing room. They all jump up.

TESMAN. She's playing with those pistols again.

TESMAN runs into the back room. HEDDA is lying over the table, dead. She has shot herself through the head, blown her brains out. Blood is everywhere – the walls, the table, the floor and over the portrait of General Gabler. HEDDA is dead, but her blood pulses out of the wound.

THEA screams. BERTHE runs in. All at once:

TESMAN (*screaming*). Hedda! Heddaaa!! (*To* BRACK.) She's shot herself! It's in the head!

THEA. No no no no no! Pleeeeease no . . . !

BERTHE. Aaaaah dear God alive!

BRACK. Oh God oh God oh God . . .

TESMAN stumbles back into the drawing room like a victim of a bomb blast. THEA shrinks from the lifeless body, sobbing.

BERTHE uses her apron to staunch the flow of blood from HEDDA's head and strokes her as if she could bring her comfort.

BRACK slumps in the armchair, shaking his head.

TESMAN (*murmuring*). Amazing . . . amazing . . .

BRACK. Oh God . . . People . . . don't . . . do things like that . . .

Fade to black.